Flowers that are mostly blue   pg. 19

Flowers that are mostly green

Flowers that are mostly orange   pg. 59

Flowers that have prominent pink   pg. 71

Flowers that are mostly purple   pg. 161

Flowers that are mostly red   pg. 225

Flowers that are mostly white   pg. 245

Flowers that are mostly yellow   pg. 315

T0273558

2ND EDITION

Wildflowers
of Texas
Field Guide

Nora Mays Bowers,
Rick Bowers,
and Stan Tekiela

PUBLICATIONS
Adventure
an imprint of AdventureKEEN

Dedication

To my husband, Rick, because his love of nature is as big as Texas —Nora

To Matt Johnson, who always kept plants on my mind and taught me so much about them —Rick

To my daughter, Abigail Rose, the sweetest flower in my life —Stan

Acknowledgments

Nora and Rick would like to thank Stan Tekiela and Deborah Walsh for their generosity and support, without which this book would not have been possible.

A very special thanks to the following people and institutions who shared their knowledge of plants or allowed us to photograph wildflowers: Matt Johnson at the Desert Legume Project, University of Arizona; Cathryn Hoyt, Mileniusz Spanowicz and Marc Goff at the Chihuahuan Desert Research Institute, Fort Davis, Texas; Daniel Moerman for the Native American Ethnobotany web site, University of Michigan-Dearborn; Angelica Elliott at the Desert Botanical Garden, Phoenix, Arizona; Franklin Mountain State Park, El Paso, Texas; Flora of North America website; and Riverside Nature Center, Kerrville, Texas. Thanks also to Bill Carr at the Lady Bird Johnson Wildflower Center in Austin, Texas, for reviewing the book.

Edited by Deborah Walsh

Book and icon design by Jonathan Norberg

Cover photo: Virginia Iris by Rick and Nora Bowers.
See pages 428 for photo credits by photographer and page number.

10 9 8 7 6 5 4 3 2

Wildflowers of Texas Field Guide
First Edition 2009, Second Edition 2023
Copyright © 2009 and 2023 by Nora Mays Bowers, Rick Bowers, and Stan Tekiela
Published by Adventure Publications
An imprint of AdventureKEEN
310 Garfield Street South
Cambridge, Minnesota 55008
(800) 678–7006
www.adventurepublications.net
LCCN 2022042975 (print); 2022042976 (ebook)
ISBN 978–1–64755–382–1 (pbk.); ISBN 978–1–64755–383–8 (ebook)

TABLE OF CONTENTS

Introduction

Texas and Wildflowers. 6
Strategies for Identifying Wildflowers 6
Using the Icons. 8
Blooming Season 12
Life Cycle/Origin 13
Habitats. 14
Range 14
Notes 14
Caution 14

Sample Pages 16–17

The Wildflowers

Flowers That Are Mostly Blue. 19
Flowers That Are Mostly Green 57
Flowers That Are Mostly Orange 59
Flowers That Have Prominent Pink. 71
Flowers That Are Mostly Purple. 161
Flowers That Are Mostly Red 225
Flowers That Are Mostly White 245
Flowers That Are Mostly Yellow. 315

Glossary 418

Checklist/Index by Species 423

Photo Credits 428

About the Authors 430

TEXAS AND WILDFLOWERS

Texas is a great place for wildflower enthusiasts! From the arid desert in the far west to the moist pine and deciduous forests in the east, and from the prairies and hills of the central part of the state to the subtropical climate in the south, Texas is fortunate to have an extremely diverse, often unique, and very healthy variety of wonderful wildflowers.

Wildflowers of Texas Field Guide is an easy-to-use field guide to help the curious nature seeker identify 200 of the most common and widespread wildflowers in the state. It features, with a number of exceptions, the herbaceous wildflowers of Texas. Herbaceous plants have green soft stems and die back to the ground each autumn. Some plants with woody stems have been included because these particular plants are very common and have large, showy flowers.

Wildflowers of Texas Field Guide is one in a series of five unique field guides for Texas, including those for birds, mammals, trees, and cacti.

STRATEGIES FOR IDENTIFYING WILDFLOWERS

Determining the color of the flower is the first step in a simple five-step process to identify a wildflower.

Because this guide is organized by color, identifying an unknown wildflower is as simple as matching the color of the flower to the color section of the book. The color tabs on each page identify the color section.

The second step in determining the identity of a wildflower is to note the size. Within each color section, the flowers are arranged by the size of the flower, or flower cluster, from small to large. A plant with a single, small, yellow flower will be in the beginning of the yellow section, while a large white flower will be towards the end of the white section. Sometimes flowers are made up of many individual flowers in clusters that are perceived to be one larger flower. Therefore, these will be ordered by the size of the cluster, not the individual flower. See page 432 for rulers to help estimate flower and leaf size.

Once you have determined the color and approximate size, observe the appearance of the flower. Is it a single flower or cluster of flowers? If it is a cluster, is the general shape of the cluster flat, round, or spike? For the single flowers, note if the flower has a regular, irregular, bell, or tube shape. Also, counting the number of petals might help to identify these individual flowers. Compare your findings with the descriptions on each page. Examining the flower as described above should result in narrowing the identity of the wildflower down to just a few candidates.

The fourth step is to look at the leaves. There are several possible shapes or types of leaves. Simple leaves have only one leaf blade but can be lobed. Compound leaves have a long central leaf stalk with many smaller leaflets attached. Twice compound leaves have two or more leaf stalks and many leaflets. Sometimes it is helpful to note if the leaves have toothed or smooth margins (edges), so look for this also.

For the fifth step, check to see how the leaf is attached to the stem. Some plants may look similar but have different leaf attachments, so this can be very helpful. Look to see if the leaves are attached opposite of each other along the stem, alternately, or whorled around a point on the stem. Sometimes the leaves occur at the base of the plant (basal). Some leaves do not have a leaf stalk and clasp the stem at their base (clasping), and in some cases the stem appears to pass through the base of the leaf (perfoliate).

Using these five steps (color, size, shape, leaves, and leaf attachment) will help you gather the clues needed to quickly and easily identify the common wildflowers of Texas.

USING THE ICONS

Sometimes the botanical terms for leaf type, attachment, and type of flower can be confusing and difficult to remember. Because of this, we have included icons at the bottom of each page. They can be used to quickly and visually match the main features of the plant to the specimen you are viewing even if you don't completely understand the botanical terms. By using the photos, text descriptions, and icons in this field guide, you should be able to quickly and easily identify most of the common wildflowers of Texas.

The icons are arranged from left to right in the following order: flower cluster type, flower type, leaf type, leaf attachment, and fruit. The first two flower icons refer to cluster type and flower type. While these are not botanically separate categories, we have made separate icons for them to simplify identification.

Flower Cluster Icons

     (icon color is dependent on flower color)

Flat   Round   Spike

Any cluster (tightly formed group) of flowers can be categorized into one of three cluster types based on its overall shape. The flat, round, and spike types refer to the cluster shape, which is easy to observe. Technically there is another cluster type, composite, which appears as a single daisy-like flower but is actually a cluster of many tiny flowers. Because this is often perceived as a flower type, we have included the icon in the flower type section. See page 9 for its description.

Some examples of cluster types

Flat   Round   Spike

Flower Type Icons

(icon color is dependent on flower color)

Regular   Irregular   Bell   Tube   Composite

Botanically speaking, there are many types of flowers, but in this guide, we are simplifying them to five basic types. Regular flowers are defined as having a round shape with three or more petals, lacking a disk-like center. Irregular flowers are not round but uniquely shaped with fused petals. Bell flowers are hanging with fused petals. Tube flowers are longer and narrower than bell flowers and point up. Composite flowers (technically a flower cluster) are usually round compact clusters of tiny flowers appearing as one larger flower.

Some examples of flower types

Regular   **Irregular**   **Bell**

disk flowers
ray flowers

Tube   **Composite**

Composite cluster: Although a composite flower is technically a type of flower cluster, we are including the icon in the flower type category since most people who are unfamiliar with botany would visually see it as a flower type, not a flower cluster. A composite flower consists of petals (ray flowers) and/or a round disk-like center (disk flowers). Sometimes a flower has only ray flowers, sometimes only disk flowers or both.

Leaf Type Icons

Simple **Simple Lobed** **Compound** **Twice Compound** **Palmate** **Spines**

Leaf type can be broken down into two main types: simple and compound. Simple leaves are leaves that are in one piece; the leaf is not divided into smaller leaflets. It can have teeth or be smooth along the edges. The simple leaf is depicted by the simple leaf icon. Simple leaves may have lobes and sinuses that give the leaf a unique shape. These simple leaves with lobes are depicted by the simple lobed icon.

Some examples of leaf types

Simple **Simple Lobed** **Compound**

Twice Compound **Palmate** **Spines**

Compound leaves have two or more distinct, small leaves called leaflets that arise from a single stalk. In this field guide we are dividing compound leaves into regular compound, twice compound, or palmately compound leaves. Twice compound leaves are those that have many distinct leaflets arising from a secondary leaf stalk. Palmately compound leaves are those with three or more leaflets arising from a common central point.

Leaf Attachment Icons

Alternate **Opposite** **Whorl** **Clasping** **Perfoliate** **Basal**

Leaves attach to the stems in different ways. There are six main types of attachment, but a plant can have two different types of attachments. This is most often seen in the combination of basal leaves and leaves that attach along the main stem either alternate or opposite (cauline leaves). These wildflowers have some leaves at the base of the plant, usually in a rosette pattern, and some leaves along the stem. In these cases, both icons are included; for most plants, there will only be one leaf attachment icon.

Some examples of leaf attachment

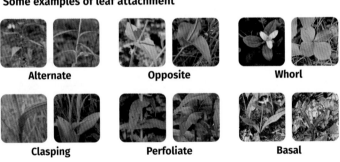

Alternate   **Opposite**   **Whorl**

Clasping   **Perfoliate**   **Basal**

Alternate leaves attach to the stem in an alternating pattern, while opposite leaves attach to the stem directly opposite from each other. Whorled leaves have three or more leaves that attach around the stem at the same point. Clasping leaves have no stalk, and the base of the leaf partly surrounds the main stem. Perfoliate leaves are also stalkless and have a leaf base that completely surrounds the main stem. Basal leaves are those that originate at the base of a plant, near the ground, usually grouped in a round rosette.

Fruit Icons

  (icon color is dependent on berry or pod color)

Berry Pod

In some flower descriptions a fruit category has been included. This may be especially useful when a plant is not in bloom or when the fruit is particularly large or otherwise noteworthy. Botanically speaking, there are many types of fruit. We have simplified these often-confusing fruit categories into two general groups, berry and pod.

Some examples of fruit types

Berry   **Pod**

The berry icon is used to depict a soft, fleshy, often-round structure containing seeds. The pod icon is used to represent a dry structure that, when mature, splits open to release seeds.

BLOOMING SEASON

Most wildflowers have a specific season of blooming. You probably won't see, for example, the common spring-blooming Spring Beauty blooming in summer or fall. Knowing the season of bloom can help you narrow your selection as you try to identify an unknown flower. In this field guide, spring usually refers to early March, April, and the first half of May, although several flowers, including Tenpetal Thimbleweed, bloom as early as January in some areas of the state. Summer means late May, June, July, and August. Fall usually means September and October, but it includes November in southern Texas.

LIFE CYCLE/ORIGIN

The life cycle of a wildflower describes how long a wildflower lives. Annual wildflowers are short-lived. They sprout, grow, and bloom in only one season, never to return except from seed. Most wildflowers have perennial life cycles that last many years. Perennial wildflowers are usually deeply rooted plants that grow from the roots each year. They return each year from their roots, but they also produce seeds to start other perennial plants. Similar to the annual life cycle is the biennial cycle. This group of plants takes two seasons of growth to bloom. The first year, the plant produces a low growth of basal leaves. During the second year, the plant sends up a flower stalk from which it produces seeds, from which new plants can be started. However, the original plant will not return for a third year of growth.

Origin indicates whether the plants are native or nonnative. Most of the wildflowers in this book originate in Texas and are considered native plants. Nonnative plants were often introduced unintentionally when they escaped from gardens or farms. The nonnative plants in this book are now naturalized in Texas.

Some plants are also considered invasive (nonnative and capable of destructive spread) or noxious (detrimental to the environment, people, or economy). Learn more about the problem plants and other invasives in Texas by visiting www.tsusinvasives.org.

HABITATS

Some wildflowers thrive only in specific habitats. They may require certain types of soil, moisture, pH levels, fungi, or nutrients. Other wildflowers are generalists and can grow just about anywhere. Sometimes noting the habitat surrounding the flower in question can be a clue to its identity.

RANGE

The wide variety of habitats in Texas naturally restricts the range of certain wildflowers that have specific requirements. For example, a wildflower such as Blue Mistflower that requires moist soils may only be found along roadside ditches, pond edges, and shady stream banks in eastern Texas. Sometimes this section can help you eliminate a wildflower from consideration just based on its range. However, please keep in mind that the ranges indicated are general notations on where the flower is commonly found. They are general guidelines only, and there will certainly be exceptions to these ranges.

NOTES

The Notes are fun and fact-filled with many interesting "gee-whiz" tidbits of information such as historical uses, other common names, insect relationship, color variations, and much more. Much of the information in this section cannot be found in other wildflower field guides.

CAUTION

In the Notes, it is mentioned that in some cultures, some of the wildflowers were used for medicine or food. While some find this interesting, DO NOT use this guide to identify edible or medicinal plants. Some of the wildflowers in Texas are toxic or have toxic look-alikes that can cause severe problems. Do not take the chance of making a mistake. Please enjoy the wildflowers with your eyes or through a camera lens. In addition, please don't pick, trample, or transplant any wildflowers you see. The flower of a plant is its reproductive structure, and if you pick a flower, you have eliminated its ability to reproduce. Transplanting wildflowers is another destructive occurrence. Most wildflowers need specific soil types, pH levels, or special bacteria or fungi in the soil to grow properly. If you attempt to transplant a wildflower to a habitat that is not suitable for its particular needs, the wildflower most likely will die. Also, some wildflowers, due to their dwindling populations, are protected by laws that forbid you to disturb them. Many Texas wildflowers are now available at local garden centers. These wildflowers have been cultivated and have not been dug from the wild. More gardeners are taking advantage of the availability of these wildflowers, planting native species, and helping the planet.

Enjoy the wild wildflowers!

Nora, Rick, and Stan

fruit

Common Name

Scientific name

Color Indicator ——

Family: plant family name

Height: average range of mature plant

Flower: general description, type of flower, size of flower, number of petals

Leaf: general description, size, leaf type, type of attachment, toothed or smooth

Fruit: berry or pod

Bloom: spring, summer, fall

Cycle/Origin: annual, perennial, biennial, native, nonnative

Habitat: general environment in which you are likely to find the flower

Range: an approximate range where the flower is found

Stan's Notes: helpful identification information, history, origin, and other interesting, "gee-whiz" nature facts

Not all icons are found on every page. See preceding pages for icon descriptions.

CLUSTER TYPE	FLOWER TYPE	LEAF TYPE	LEAF ATTACHMENT	LEAF ATTACHMENT	FRUIT
Round	**Regular**	**Simple**	**Opposite**	**Whorl**	**Berry**

Roadside Blue-eyed Grass
Sisyrinchium langloisii

Family: Iris (Iridaceae)

Height: 4–12" (10–30 cm)

Flower: collection of blue flowers with bright-yellow centers; individual flower, ½–1" (1–2.5 cm) wide, has 6 petals, each with a yellow base and tipped with a small point; groups of flowers are on short stalks from longer, leaf-like stems

Leaf: long, thin, pointed leaves, ¼" (.6 cm) wide and up to 8" (20 cm) long, are often confused with blades of grass

Bloom: spring, early summer

Cycle/Origin: perennial; native

Habitat: moist soils, along roads, prairies, open woods

Range: eastern, coastal, southern, and central Texas

Notes: One of over 40 species of blue-eyed grass in North America, this plant is the most common of more than a dozen species in Texas. Frequently mistaken for a type of grass because of its leaves, Roadside Blue-eyed Grass is actually a member of the Iris family. Unlike some other irises, which spread by horizontal underground stems (rhizomes), this primitive iris has fibrous vertical roots. Like other irises, the blossoms are made up of three petal-like sepals and three petals. The flowers can be bluish violet or white, and the stems can sometimes be bluish purple. Historically, the young leaves were cooked and eaten to treat constipation.

FLOWER TYPE   LEAF TYPE   LEAF ATTACHMENT
Regular   **Simple**   **Basal**

Largeflower Baby Blue Eyes
Nemophila phacelioides

Family: Waterleaf (Hydrophyllaceae)

Height: 3–24" (7.5–61 cm)

Flower: bowl-shaped, sky blue-to-violet flowers, ½–1½" (1–4 cm) wide, each with 5 petals with white bases fused into a tube at base and then flaring widely

Leaf: fuzzy oak-like leaves, 1–3" (2.5–7.5 cm) long, deeply divided into 5–11 lobes with irregularly toothed edges; leaves on long stalks

Bloom: spring, early summer

Cycle/Origin: annual; native

Habitat: sandy soils in moist habitats, edges of thickets and woodlands, canyons, river bottoms, coastal brushlands, roadsides, partial shade to full sun

Range: central, southeastern, and coastal Texas

Notes: Mostly a spring bloomer, this multi-branched sprawling or upright annual does not tolerate heat well and wilts as soon as temperatures begin to rise in early summer. Usually grows in moist, shady habitats, forming quite large colonies. Although it does not thrive in dry, hot conditions, it can be found on well-drained slopes in full sun. A member of the Waterleaf family, the hairy foliage contains a clear watery sap. Plant this pretty woodland flower near water in shady garden spots. Native to Texas, Oklahoma, Arkansas, and Louisiana.

FLOWER TYPE
Regular

LEAF TYPE
Simple Lobed

LEAF ATTACHMENT
Alternate

Common Blue Violet
Viola sororia

Family: Violet (Violaceae)

Height: 4–10" (10–25 cm)

Flower: deep blue or deep violet-to-lavender flower (can be white), 1" (2.5 cm) wide, has 5 distinct petals surrounding a white center, with the 3 lower petals strongly veined; each flower on its own flower stalk

Leaf: characteristic heart-shaped leaves, 2–4" (5–10 cm) wide, are cupped upward and have edges with scalloped teeth

Fruit: cylindrical purple pod with many tiny brown seeds

Bloom: early spring

Cycle/Origin: perennial; native

Habitat: disturbed soils, moist woodlands, gardens, shade

Range: eastern third of Texas

Notes: Almost 80 distinct species of violet in North America and over 900 worldwide. Many botanists now lump together numerous violet species under the single species name sororia. Looks very similar to the other blue or purple violets, and like all violets, the flower color is highly variable. Often "pops up" in shady gardens and in lawns. Spreads mostly by underground runners, but also by seed. Leaves are high in vitamins and have been used in salads or cooked as greens.

FLOWER TYPE	LEAF TYPE	LEAF ATTACHMENT	FRUIT
Irregular	**Simple**	**Basal**	**Pod**

Whitemouth Dayflower

Commelina erecta

Family: Spiderwort (Commelinaceae)

Height: 6–24" (15–61 cm)

Flower: odd-shaped, sky-blue flower, 1" (2.5 cm) wide, with 2 broad upright blue petals, 1 lower white petal that is much smaller, and a golden center; in a group of several flowers; blooms open 1 at a time from a folded, shell-like green bract

Leaf: lance-shaped leaves, 2–6" (5–15 cm) long, are broad or narrow, hairy and rough above, and clasp the unbranched stems; each leaf has a prominent middle vein

Bloom: year-round, except when very cold in winter

Cycle/Origin: perennial; native

Habitat: rocky limestone hillsides, gardens, disturbed areas

Range: throughout

Notes: A widespread perennial, native to the Americas, Africa, and western Asia. Variable, it has broad or narrow leaves on upright or sprawling stems that bear a small group of buds on top, with only a single blossom open at a time. Blooms in the morning and closes early. Flowers have three petals, but only two petals are obvious and appear like ears above the third lower white petal, which is small and inconspicuous. "Whitemouth" refers to the lower petal. A preferred plant of White-tailed Deer; also eaten by livestock. Quail and doves eat the seeds. Can be invasive, spreading by seeds and tubers.

FLOWER TYPE
Irregular

LEAF TYPE
Simple

LEAF ATTACHMENT
Alternate

LEAF ATTACHMENT
Clasping

LEAF ATTACHMENT
Basal

Garden Cornflower
Centaurea cyanus

Family: Aster (Asteraceae)

Height: 8–30" (20–76 cm)

Flower: pure-blue (sometimes magenta, pink, or white) flower head, 1" (2.5 cm) wide, of disk flowers only; feathery, magenta-tipped green bracts cup the flower head; 1 flower head atop each branch; 25–100 ragged flower heads per plant

Leaf: long and narrow leaves, 5" (13 cm) long, have smooth or shallow-toothed margins or have small lobes; grayish-green stems are streaked with red

Bloom: summer

Cycle/Origin: annual; nonnative

Habitat: dry or disturbed soils, pastures, roadsides, sun

Range: throughout

Notes: This frequently cultivated flower is found in many wildflower seed mixes. A native of Europe, it has escaped from gardens to almost everywhere in the United States and Canada, growing wherever there are disturbed soils. Ironically, now rare and endangered in Great Britain. Also called Bachelor's Button, referring to its use in Old England by single women to signal marital availability. Treasured for its rare pure-blue color, this pretty bloom is used in dried flower arrangements. The blue color is due to protocyanin, a pigment that is red in roses. American Goldfinches love the ripe seeds, gracing gardens with their happy activity.

FLOWER TYPE **Composite**   LEAF TYPE **Simple**   LEAF ATTACHMENT **Alternate**

Blue Waterleaf
Hydrolea ovata

Family: Waterleaf (Hydrophyllaceae)

Height: 12–30" (30–76 cm)

Flower: upright blue or purple flower, 1" (2.5 cm) wide, has 5 pointed, widely spreading petals fused at the base and a white center with protruding purple flower parts (stamens); flowers grouped at top of stem or in leaf junctions

Leaf: broad oval leaves, 1–2½" (2.5–6 cm) long, are softly hairy with smooth margins and are stalkless or with short stalks; stout spine is below each leaf

Bloom: late summer, fall

Cycle/Origin: perennial; native

Habitat: wet soils, swamps, meadows, woods, edges of lakes or rivers, near stock tanks

Range: central, eastern, and coastal Texas

Notes: An upright or sprawling perennial with spiny stems that branch in the upper portions. One of the showiest of the late summer wildflowers in wet habitats such as stream edges or roadside ditches. Frequently found in stands near livestock ponds. Occurs in large patches, spreading from thick underground stems (rhizomes) that can tolerate being underwater for long periods of time. Cultivated in bog or water gardens for the bright-blue flowers and used by preserve managers in restoring wetlands. Ranges from Texas northeast to Missouri and Kentucky, and throughout the Southeast.

FLOWER TYPE LEAF TYPE LEAF ATTACHMENT
Regular   **Simple**   **Alternate**

Common Selfheal
Prunella vulgaris

Family: Mint (Lamiaceae)

Height: 6–12" (15–30 cm)

Flower: thick compact spike cluster, 1–2" (2.5–5 cm) long, of blue-violet flowers; each flower, ½–¾" (1–2 cm) long, is made up of 5 fused petals forming upper and lower petals (lips); upper lip forms a "hood" over the paler blue, fringed lower lip

Leaf: lance-shaped leaves, 1–3" (2.5–7.5 cm) long, are toothless, on short stalks; leaves sometimes have tiny wing-like leaves, ⅓" (.8 cm) long, growing from point of attachment; upright 4–angled stem

Bloom: spring, summer

Cycle/Origin: perennial; nonnative

Habitat: wet to moist soils, disturbed areas, pastures, lawns, fields, along streams, edges of woods

Range: far eastern Texas

Notes: Also known as Heal-all. It is used in folk medicine by many cultures throughout the world. Most commonly used in throat remedies, but little evidence of its effectiveness exists. Preferring light shade, Common Selfheal will grow in large patches in lawns and adapt to being mowed to a height of 2 inches (5 cm). Like most other members of the Mint family, Common Selfheal has a square stem; opposing leaves; and emits a faint, minty aroma when crushed. The lower lip of the flower acts as a landing platform for insects.

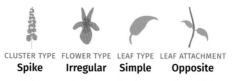

CLUSTER TYPE	FLOWER TYPE	LEAF TYPE	LEAF ATTACHMENT
Spike	**Irregular**	**Simple**	**Opposite**

Prairie Spiderwort

Tradescantia occidentalis

Family: Spiderwort (Commelinaceae)

Height: 10–30" (25–76 cm)

Flower: cluster of up to 10 flowers, each 1–2" (2.5–5 cm) wide, with 3 violet-blue petals surrounding a golden-yellow center; flowers open only a few at a time and are sometimes pink to white

Leaf: grass-like, arching, bluish-green leaves, 6–15" (15–37.5 cm) long, clasp the stem at the base; each leaf has long parallel veining and is folded lengthwise, forming a V-shaped groove

Bloom: spring, summer

Cycle/Origin: perennial; native

Habitat: disturbed areas, prairies, woodlands, along roads

Range: throughout

Notes: Unusual-looking plant with exotic-looking flowers. Flowers open in the morning and often wilt by noon on hot days. "Spider" comes from several characteristics unique to the plant. One is the angular leaf attachment, suggestive of the legs of a sitting spider; another is the stringy, mucilaginous sap that strings out like a spider's web when the leaf is torn apart. "Wort" is derived from wyrt, an Old English word for "plant." Flowers change from blue to purple when exposed to air pollution, thus it has recently been used as a natural barometer for air quality.

FLOWER TYPE	LEAF TYPE	LEAF ATTACHMENT	LEAF ATTACHMENT
Regular	**Simple**	**Alternate**	**Clasping**

Showy Prairie Gentian
Eustoma exaltatum

Family: Gentian (Gentianaceae)

Height: 6–28" (15–71 cm)

Flower: large star-shaped bloom, 2½" (6 cm) wide; blue, pink, lavender, or all white; has 5 widely spreading, wedge-shaped petals fused at white bases that are splotched pink or purple; yellow and green center

Leaf: oval, waxy, bluish-green leaves, ¾–3" (2–7.5 cm) long, with conspicuous middle veins; each pair of leaves clasping the smooth, bluish-green stem is rotated at right angles to next pair

Bloom: summer, fall

Cycle/Origin: annual, perennial; native

Habitat: moist soils, prairies, meadows, stream banks, edges of ponds, abandoned fields

Range: scattered throughout Texas

Notes: Sometimes called Catchfly Prairie Gentian or Texas Bluebells. Ranges from Texas north through the Great Plains to Montana and from California east to Florida. Also extends farther south through the West Indies and Mexico to South America. Eustoma, from the Greek eu for "good" and stoma for "mouth," refers to the wide throat formed by the fused petals. Exaltatum means "tall." A very popular wildflower in cultivation, especially in Japan, where varieties of different colors have been bred for the past 70 years. Please don't pick from the wild—there is seed available for purchase.

FLOWER TYPE	LEAF TYPE	LEAF ATTACHMENT	LEAF ATTACHMENT
Regular	**Simple**	**Opposite**	**Clasping**

Prairie Pleatleaf
Nemastylis geminiflora

Family: Iris (Iridaceae)

Height: 5–18" (13–45 cm)

Flower: blue or lavender (sometimes all-white) flowers, 2½" (6 cm) wide; each blossom has 6 petals with a darker blue and white base around yellow flower parts; groups of 1–3 flowers atop slim flower stalks

Leaf: flexible grass-like basal leaves, up to 16" (40 cm) long, are folded lengthwise and have conspicuous veins and pointed tips; usually 3 leaves per plant

Fruit: oval green capsule, turning brown, 1" (2.5 cm) long, contains many rust-colored seeds

Bloom: spring, early summer

Cycle/Origin: perennial; native

Habitat: black soil prairies, open oak woods, full sun

Range: eastern half of Texas

Notes: A perennial with beautiful delicate flowers blooming briefly in spring. Like the common garden iris, this native sprouts from a bulb. It doesn't have the irregular-shaped flower of garden iris, but rather has 6 pointed, similar-looking petals. Opens before noon and fades in late afternoon. Can form colorful dense colonies when growing in the rich black soils of prairies. "Pleatleaf" is for the folded or pleated grass-like leaf. Also known as Prairie Celestial Lily or Prairie Iris. Cultivate in wildflower meadows from bulbs purchased from garden centers selling native flowers.

FLOWER TYPE **Regular**   LEAF TYPE **Simple**   LEAF ATTACHMENT **Basal**   FRUIT **Pod**

Mealycup Sage
Salvia farinacea

Family: Mint (Lamiaceae)

Height: 12–36" (30–91 cm)

Flower: dense spike, 2–6" (5–15 cm) long, whorls of soft-blue flowers; each bloom, 1" (2.5 cm) long, has 5 fused petals forming a tube (corolla), fuzzy upper and 3–lobed lower petals (lips), and a white-haired, lavender-blue calyx; lower lip has 2 white stripes

Leaf: fuzzy, lance-shaped, grayish-green leaves, 1–3½" (2.5–9 cm) long, on long stalks, have coarse-toothed edges and pointed tips drooping or curling under; more abundant leaves lower on square, white stem

Fruit: brown pod contains 4 dark-brown nutlets

Bloom: early spring, summer, fall

Cycle/Origin: perennial; native

Habitat: limestone soils, prairies, chaparral, edges of woods, roadsides, abandoned pastures, sun

Range: southern, central, and western Texas

Notes: Farinacea is for the felt-like white hairs covering the stems, leaves, and calyx of the flower. "Sage" refers to the pungent scent, which is stronger when the foliage is wet. Hummingbirds and butterflies love the nectar, and goldfinches eat the seeds. Native to the Southwest in the wild, but naturalized in other states, where it has escaped cultivation. This wildflower is drought-tolerant and reseeds readily in colder climates, so it often is used in border plantings.

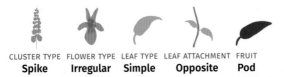

CLUSTER TYPE	FLOWER TYPE	LEAF TYPE	LEAF ATTACHMENT	FRUIT
Spike	**Irregular**	**Simple**	**Opposite**	**Pod**

Virginia Iris
Iris virginica

Family: Iris (Iridaceae)

Height: 12–36" (30–91 cm)

Flower: pale-blue or lavender-to-pinkish-white flowers, each 3" (7.5 cm) wide, with 3 horizontal drooping petal-like sepals with a pale-yellow streak on white bases and 3 smaller, upward-curving, solid-colored petals; all have dark-purple veins; 2–6 flowers per stalk

Leaf: flat and flexible, sword-shaped leaves, 15–40" (38–102 cm) long, bright-green with smooth, light-green margin and pointed tips that sometimes droop; 2–4 leaves per plant

Fruit: 3–parted elliptical green capsule, turning brown, 2" (5 cm) long

Bloom: late spring, summer

Cycle/Origin: perennial; native

Habitat: wet soils, meadows, freshwater and brackish marshes, along streams

Range: far eastern Texas

Notes: Virginia Iris can form colorful, dense colonies when growing in rich soils. Water loving, it is most common near streams or in swamps. Often planted near garden ponds, this fragrant and hardy flower is easily cultivated. Used medicinally by Cherokee Indians, but the roots are poisonous without proper preparation. Some people will develop a rash after touching the foliage.

FLOWER TYPE
Irregular

LEAF TYPE
Simple

LEAF ATTACHMENT
Basal

FRUIT
Pod

Sandyland Bluebonnet

Lupinus subcarnosus

Family: Pea or Bean (Fabaceae)

Height: 6–16" (15–40 cm)

Flower: loose spike cluster, 3–4" (7.5 cm) long, of widely spaced, pea-like, bright-blue flowers; each flower has a large white spot on the upper petal

Leaf: hand-shaped fuzzy leaves, 1–1½" (2.5–4 cm) wide, have 5 slender oval leaflets, each with a blunt tip and tiny point; long, velvety green stems rise from near the base

Fruit: upright pea-like green pod, turning tan, ¾" (2 cm) long, is oval and flat, covered with short fuzzy hairs

Bloom: spring

Cycle/Origin: annual; native

Habitat: sandy soils, abandoned fields, open woodlands

Range: southern and southeastern Texas

Notes: All six species of Lupinus found in Texas are together considered the official state flower, Bluebonnet. Sandyland Bluebonnet is aptly named since it is restricted to deep sandy soils in southern and southeastern Texas, while Texas Bluebonnet (pg. 53) is more widespread across the state. Sandyland lacks the conspicuous white tip of each flower spike characteristic of Texas Bluebonnet. The spike blooms from the bottom up, with the white spot on the standard of each pea-like flower turning magenta after pollination.

CLUSTER TYPE
Spike

FLOWER TYPE
Irregular

LEAF TYPE
Palmate

LEAF ATTACHMENT
Alternate

LEAF ATTACHMENT
Basal

FRUIT
Pod

Pickerelweed
Pontederia cordata

Family: Pickerelweed (Pontederiaceae)

Height: aquatic

Flower: spike cluster, 4–6" (10–15 cm) long, of small blue-to-violet flowers; each irregular, but somewhat tubular flower has 6 petals (1 upper petal has 2 yellow spots)

Leaf: heart- or lance-shaped leaves, 4–10" (10–25 cm) long and ½–6" (1–15 cm) wide, have parallel veins, are glossy, toothless, and indented at base where stalk attaches; leaves rise from an underwater root

Bloom: summer, fall

Cycle/Origin: perennial; native

Habitat: shallow quiet edges of lakes, wetlands, ponds, streams, wet roadside ditches, freshwater marshes

Range: eastern half of Texas

Notes: Pickerelweed is an aquatic plant rooted to the bottoms of bodies of fresh water or wet areas. Its leaves and flowers protrude above the water. Forms large colonies, spreading by short underground stems (rhizomes). Preferring shallow water, pickerelweed helps filter polluted water in marshes. Common name refers to the Pickerel, a fish that shares a similar aquatic habitat. Pickerelweed is a good choice for a water garden. Its young leaves are edible in salads, and the roasted or dried seeds are nutritious.

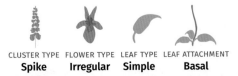

CLUSTER TYPE	FLOWER TYPE	LEAF TYPE	LEAF ATTACHMENT
Spike	**Irregular**	**Simple**	**Basal**

Blue Mistflower
Conoclinium coelestinum

Family: Aster (Asteraceae)

Height: 12–36" (30–91 cm)

Flower: disk-shaped flat cluster, 4–8" (10–20 cm) wide, of lilac blue-to-pale-purple flower heads; each flower head is made up of 40–70 tubular disk flowers that are cupped by pointed green bracts with burgundy tips

Leaf: arrowhead-shaped leaves, 2–4" (5–10 cm) long, are deeply grooved above and have round-toothed margins; lower leaves are smaller than upper leaves; oppositely attached to single fuzzy green or red stem

Bloom: spring, summer, fall

Cycle/Origin: perennial; native

Habitat: moist soils, thickets, shady stream banks, roadside ditches, pond edges

Range: eastern half of Texas

Notes: Blue Mistflower is similar to plants in the genus *Ageratum*, and is sometimes called Wild Ageratum. Frequently cultivated in butterfly and perennial gardens, producing eye-catching blooms when planted in masses. Attracts large, colorful butterflies, such as Monarchs, Painted Ladies, or Common Buckeyes, that stop for a nectar break on their way south in the fall. In addition, the males of Monarch and Queen butterflies need an alkaloid found in the nectar to make pheromones for attracting mates. This bitter alkaloid is avoided by deer and rabbits.

CLUSTER TYPE	FLOWER TYPE	LEAF TYPE	LEAF ATTACHMENT
Flat	**Composite**	**Simple**	**Opposite**

Azure Blue Sage
Salvia azurea

Family: Mint (Lamiaceae)

Height: 3–5' (.9–1.5 m)

Flower: spike cluster, 4–12" (10–30 cm) long, of groups of 1–4 pale light-blue-to-deep-blue or purple flowers; each flower, 1" (2.5 cm) long, has petals fused to form a long tube (corolla) and small arched upper and broader lower petals (lips)

Leaf: variable-shaped leaves (can be oval, oblong, or lance-shaped), 3–4" (7.5–10 cm) long, with edges smooth or toothed; upper leaves are smaller

Fruit: cup-shaped, reddish-brown pod contains dimpled, dark-brown nutlets

Bloom: summer, fall

Cycle/Origin: perennial; native

Habitat: dry rocky soils, prairies, limestone glades, roadsides

Range: throughout Texas, except the far western part of the state

Notes: A stately, long-blooming, tough plant that can be sown in wildflower meadows. Tolerates full sun, but flower color deepens with more shade. Although in the Mint family, the foliage does not smell or taste minty–it has an aromatic scent and is avoided by deer. One of the tallest native sages, which are also commonly referred to as salvias. Native to the southern and western prairie states. Can be found in tallgrass prairies in small colonies.

CLUSTER TYPE	FLOWER TYPE	LEAF TYPE	LEAF ATTACHMENT	FRUIT
Spike	**Irregular**	**Simple**	**Opposite**	**Pod**

Atlantic Camas
Camassia scilloides

Family: Lily (Liliaceae)

Height: 6–32" (15–80 cm)

Flower: tall spike cluster, 5–7" (13–18 cm) long, of star-shaped, pale-blue or lavender (sometimes all-white) flowers; each blossom, 1" (2.5 cm) wide, has 6 pointed petals around green-and-white spreading flower parts; blooms at bottom of spike open first

Leaf: flexible grass-like basal leaves, 8–16" (20–40 cm) long; each leaf has a conspicuously lighter green middle vein and a pointed tip

Fruit: 3–parted, reddish-green capsule, 1" (2.5 cm) long, turns reddish brown when mature and each part opens at the top, revealing many shiny black seeds

Bloom: spring

Cycle/Origin: perennial; native

Habitat: black soil prairies, pastures, open woods, roadsides

Range: central and eastern Texas

Notes: Also called Wild Hyacinth. Forms large colonies in the wild and is often included in prairie restorations. Historically, people dug up and roasted the bulbs to eat. The genus name is from an American Indian word for "sweet," describing the taste of the bulbs. Reportedly a favorite food of grizzly bears, which once ranged into Texas. Sadly, grizzlies no longer occur in the range of this wildflower.

CLUSTER TYPE	FLOWER TYPE	LEAF TYPE	LEAF ATTACHMENT	FRUIT
Spike	**Regular**	**Simple**	**Basal**	**Pod**

Texas Bluebonnet
Lupinus texensis

Family: Pea or Bean (Fabaceae)

Height: 6–24" (15–61 cm)

Flower: dark-blue spike clusters, 6–8" (15–20 cm) long, with conspicuous pointed white tips and many fragrant pea-like flowers, each with a white spot on upper petal that turns magenta after pollination

Leaf: hand-shaped, grayish-green leaves, 1–2" (2.5–5 cm) wide, have 5–7 slender oval leaflets with pointed tips; long, velvety green stems rise from base

Fruit: very fuzzy, flat, pea-like pod; 1–1½" (2.5–4 cm) long, green turning tan

Bloom: spring, early summer

Cycle/Origin: annual; native

Habitat: prairies, roadsides, hillsides, fields

Range: eastern, southern, and central Texas

Notes: This wildflower carpets whole fields blue in spring, especially in the limestone soils of the hills of central Texas. A favorite planted by the highway department and garden clubs, it is the most common lupine seen along highways. Prefers to grow in poor or disturbed soils, as it can fix nitrogen from the air, adding to soil fertility. Plant it in fall; it will sprout a rosette of leaves that remains on the plant in winter and blooms in spring. Elf butterfly caterpillars eat the foliage, which is densely covered with tiny, silvery white hairs.

CLUSTER TYPE
Spike

FLOWER TYPE
Irregular

LEAF TYPE
Palmate

LEAF ATTACHMENT
Alternate

LEAF ATTACHMENT
Basal

FRUIT
Pod

53

leaf

Carolina Larkspur

Delphinium carolinianum

Family: Buttercup (Ranunculaceae)

Height: 3–5' (.9–1.5 m)

Flower: open loose spike cluster, 8–12" (20–30 cm) long, of blue-and-purple flowers; each bloom, 1" (2.5 cm) wide, has 5 blue petal-like sepals (upper sepal with long, backward-curving, purplish-white spur) and 4 smaller, hairy purple petals in center (upper 2 petals have small spurs); flowers can be white

Leaf: narrow, irregularly lobed leaves, 3½" (9 cm) long; lower leaves on long stalks, upper leaves nearly stalkless; long, slender, fuzzy stem; basal rosette forming in winter usually wilts before plant flowers

Bloom: spring, summer

Cycle/Origin: perennial; native

Habitat: fields, rangelands, prairies, clearings in woodlands

Range: throughout, except the far western part of Texas

Notes: Beautiful and easily grown, this perennial can cover acres of prairies in the spring, when most of the native grasses are still dormant. Extremely toxic, especially to young children who may be tempted to suck on the flower spur for the nectar. Cattle have been killed by consuming the plant when forage is scarce. The seeds were used by Plains Indians to fill ceremonial gourd rattles, and ground-up seeds were mixed with alcohol to use as flea repellent. Originally discovered in the Carolinas, thus the first part of the common name.

CLUSTER TYPE
Spike

FLOWER TYPE
Irregular

LEAF TYPE
Simple Lobed

LEAF ATTACHMENT
Alternate

LEAF ATTACHMENT
Basal

fruit

Spider Milkweed

Asclepias asperula

Family: Milkweed (Asclepiadaceae)

Height: 12–24" (30–61 cm)

Flower: round cluster, 3" (7.5 cm) wide, of pale green-and-dark-purple flowers; each bloom, ½" (1 cm) wide, has 5 upward-curving petals and a 5–part crown of purple horns tipped with white

Leaf: narrow triangular leaves, 4–6" (10–15 cm) long, are dark green with a reddish-green middle vein and have pointed tips and wavy edges that curl upward

Fruit: stout curved conical pod, 6" (15 cm) long, is green with pink streaks and has deep lengthwise wrinkles and a pointed tip; contains flat brown seeds

Bloom: spring, summer, fall

Cycle/Origin: perennial; native

Habitat: deserts, open areas in woodlands, fields, prairies, flats, slopes, along sandy washes and highways

Range: throughout

Notes: Pairs of conical pods resemble the curved horns of Pronghorn Antelope, thus it is also often called Antelope Horns. Inside the pod, teardrop-shaped seeds are in spiral layers around hair-like white fuzz that carries the seeds away on the wind. The foliage, which contains alkaloids, is eaten by Monarch butterfly caterpillars, rendering them and the resulting butterflies poisonous to predators.

CLUSTER TYPE	FLOWER TYPE	LEAF TYPE	LEAF ATTACHMENT	FRUIT
Round	**Irregular**	**Simple**	**Alternate**	**Pod**

Berlandier Flax
Linum berlandieri

Family: Flax (Linaceae)

Height: 8–20" (20–50 cm)

Flower: coppery orange flowers, 1–1½" (2.5–4 cm) wide; each has 5 broad fan-shaped petals with reddish-brown bases around a green-and-orange center; blossoms last only 1 day

Leaf: stalkless narrow leaves, 1⅜" (3.5 cm) long, with sharply pointed tips, are alternately attached; densely leafy, stiffly upright stems

Bloom: spring, summer

Cycle/Origin: annual, perennial; native

Habitat: prairies, fields, woodland edges, disturbed rocky ground, sun

Range: scattered throughout Texas

Notes: The genus name Linum is from an old Greek name for "flax," which are important plants that produce a thread used to weave linen cloth. There are over 20 species of flax in Texas, many with orange or yellow flowers. This small, upright wildflower is a host plant for the caterpillars of Variegated Fritillary, a medium-size butterfly. Often planted in butterfly or wildflower gardens since it is easy to grow from seed. The seeds are ignored by most birds, except House Finches and Mourning Doves.

FLOWER TYPE
Regular

LEAF TYPE
Simple

LEAF ATTACHMENT
Alternate

fruit

Texas Lantana
Lantana urticoides

Family: Verbena (Verbenaceae)

Height: 3–5' (.9–1.5 m); shrub

Flower: orange-and-yellow round cluster, 1–3" (2.5–7.5 cm) wide, of tiny yellow flowers with 5 rounded petals that turn orange, then red as they age; flowers open on outside edge first; unopened buds are square

Leaf: rough, lance-shaped leaves, 1–2½" (2.5–6 cm) long, are aromatic, crinkled, grayish-green, and coarsely toothed; woody stem becomes thorny with age

Fruit: small poisonous green berry, turning bluish black when ripe; in clusters, 1–3" (2.5–7.5 cm) wide

Bloom: spring, summer, fall

Cycle/Origin: perennial; native

Habitat: poor soils, disturbed sites, along roads, fields, thickets, swamps, sandy woods, chaparral

Range: throughout, except the northwestern part of Texas

Notes: This low, spreading shrub branches profusely near the ground. The species name *urticoides* means "stinging like a nettle," referring to star-shaped hairs covering the leaves and twigs that can cause a rash if handled. It is drought-tolerant and easily grown for its colorful flowers, which attract butterflies. Sometimes called Calicobush for the multicolored blooms. Freezes back throughout most of Texas in the winter. Cut the old stems back, as only new growth sprouts flowers.

CLUSTER TYPE
Round

FLOWER TYPE
Regular

LEAF TYPE
Simple

LEAF ATTACHMENT
Opposite

LEAF ATTACHMENT
Whorl

FRUIT
Berry

Entireleaf Indian Paintbrush

Castilleja indivisa

Family: Snapdragon (Scrophulariaceae)

Height: 12–16" (30–40 cm)

Flower: leaf-like, reddish-orange bracts in a spike cluster, 1–4" (2.5–10 cm) long, are often mistaken for flower petals; actual greenish-white flowers, 1" (2.5 cm) long, are tubular, inconspicuous, and interspersed among the bracts

Leaf: narrow, oval, grayish-green leaves, 1–4" (2.5–10 cm) long, are covered with dense white hairs, heavily veined and have wavy edges; leaves alternate at wide intervals along reddish-green stem

Fruit: small pod-like green container, ½" (1 cm) long

Bloom: early spring, summer

Cycle/Origin: annual; native

Habitat: disturbed soils, prairies, roadsides, and open grassy areas

Range: eastern half of Texas

Notes: "Paintbrush" in the common name is for the resemblance of the bracts to paintbrushes dipped in paint. Pollinated mainly by hummingbirds, which are attracted by the reddish-orange color of the bracts, but get nectar from the tubular flowers. Can be cultivated from seed, but it needs to be planted near other species to absorb nutrients from their roots (semiparasitic). Also known as Texas Paintbrush. Ranges from Texas east to Arkansas and Louisiana and north to Oklahoma.

CLUSTER TYPE	FLOWER TYPE	LEAF TYPE	LEAF ATTACHMENT	FRUIT
Spike	**Tube**	**Simple**	**Alternate**	**Pod**

Indian Blanket
Gaillardia pulchella

Family: Aster (Asteraceae)

Height: 2–24" (5–61 cm)

Flower: daisy-like tricolored flower head, 2–3" (5–7.5 cm) wide, made up of 8–14 triangular (orange, red, or purple) petals with 3–lobed (usually yellow or orange) tips surrounding a domed maroon center

Leaf: narrowly oblong or spoon-shaped leaves, ½–3½" (1–9 cm) long, are fuzzy above with usually smooth edges; upper leaves smaller and clasping; alternately attached to multi-branched, sticky-haired stem

Bloom: year-round

Cycle/Origin: annual; native

Habitat: prairies, open woodlands, fields, disturbed ground, along roads and railroads, sun

Range: throughout

Notes: Also called Firewheel because the flower resembles a child's pinwheel, with its maroon center surrounded by an orange or red ring that, in turn, is encircled by a ring of yellow. Readily self-seeds and forms large colorful masses of flowers that blanket the ground. Many state highway departments, including the Texas Department of Transportation, plant this eye-catching flower along roads. Often grown in wildflower gardens and restored prairies, since it needs little care and the flowers last a long time.

FLOWER TYPE   LEAF TYPE   LEAF ATTACHMENT
Composite   **Simple**   **Alternate**

fruit

Butterflyweed
Asclepias tuberosa

Family: Milkweed (Asclepiadaceae)

Height: 12–24" (30–61 cm)

Flower: large flat cluster, 2–3" (5–7.5 cm) wide, of small, deep-orange flowers; each flower, ⅜" (.9 cm) wide, with downward-curving petals; flower color varies from all yellow to red

Leaf: hairy lance-shaped leaves, 2–6" (5–15 cm) long, widen near tips and are toothless; hairy stem

Fruit: upright, narrow green pod, 6" (15 cm) long, turning brown, is covered with fine hairs; pods are in small clusters and have large brown seeds with silken "parachutes" to carry away each seed

Bloom: spring, summer, fall

Cycle/Origin: perennial; native

Habitat: open sandy areas, prairies, fields, dunes, hills, forest clearings, sun

Range: throughout, but especially the eastern half of Texas

Notes: Also called Butterfly Milkweed. Found in clumps, this true milkweed lacks milky sap. Instead, its stem and leaves contain clear sap. Species name tuberosa refers to its large taproot, which makes it nearly impossible to transplant. Can be grown from seed. Single stems branch only near the top, and flower clusters harbor up to 25 individual flowers. Roots and stems have been used in folk medicine. A host for Gray Hairstreak and Monarch butterfly caterpillars.

CLUSTER TYPE	FLOWER TYPE	LEAF TYPE	LEAF ATTACHMENT	FRUIT
Flat	**Irregular**	**Simple**	**Alternate**	**Pod**

Standing Cypress
Ipomopsis rubra

Family: Phlox (Polemoniaceae)

Height: 2–6' (.6–1.8 m)

Flower: dense spike cluster, 6–12" (15–30 cm) long, of reddish-orange flowers speckled dark red inside; each flower, 1½" (4 cm) long, has petals fused into a long narrow tube and flaring into 5 pointed lobes, with slender flower parts protruding from the mouth

Leaf: feathery basal leaves, ½–2" (1–5 cm) long, are deeply divided into numerous thread-like lobes; similar densely packed stem leaves

Bloom: spring, summer

Cycle/Origin: biennial; native

Habitat: dry sandy soils, abandoned pastures, edges of woods, disturbed areas

Range: central and eastern Texas

Notes: Standing Cypress is native to the eastern United States, ranging from Texas east to Florida and north to Canada. Forms large colonies with masses of flowers in the wild. A sturdy, upright wildflower that is popular with gardeners. The feathery foliage is attractive even the first year after planting, before this biennial blooms. Flowers at the top of the long spike open first. Hummingbirds are drawn to the numerous bright, reddish-orange flowers, like moths to a flame. Drought-tolerant once established, it will self-seed if planted in sandy soil.

CLUSTER TYPE
Spike

FLOWER TYPE
Tube

LEAF TYPE
Simple Lobed

LEAF ATTACHMENT
Alternate

LEAF ATTACHMENT
Basal

Poorjoe
Diodia teres

Family: Madder (Rubiaceae)

Height: 6–24" (15–61 cm)

Flower: tiny flowers, ¼" (.6 cm) long, are pale purplish pink and have 4 pointed petals fused into a short tube at their bases; 2–6 delicate-looking flowers at each leaf attachment

Leaf: slender leaves, ½–1¼" (1–3 cm) long, have pointed tips, edges rolled under, and noticeable middle veins; membranes connecting the bases of the stalkless, opposite leaves have long bristles

Bloom: summer, fall

Cycle/Origin: annual, perennial; native

Habitat: poor sandy soils, overgrazed fields, gravelly areas along roads and railroads

Range: eastern half of Texas

Notes: One of the most common weeds in Texas and found throughout the South and northeastern United States. The common name refers to its preference for disturbed areas with poor soil. A hairy, upright or sprawling annual with a single, widely branching, reddish-green stem. Has inconspicuous tiny flowers, but is easily identified by the long bristles arising from membranes at the leaf nodes. Also called Rough Buttonweed for the shape of the tiny fruit. Often found growing with Camphorweed (pg. 325).

FLOWER TYPE **Tube** LEAF TYPE **Simple** LEAF ATTACHMENT **Opposite** LEAF ATTACHMENT **Clasping**

71

Spreading Dogbane

Apocynum androsaemifolium

Family: Dogbane (Apocynaceae)

Height: 12–20" (30–50 cm)

Flower: groups of 2–10 pink-to-white flowers on stalks above leaves; each bell-shaped flower, ⅓" (.8 cm) long, can be mostly white with pink stripes within the bell

Leaf: oval leaves, 2–4" (5–10 cm) long, pale whitish green and slightly hairy below, toothless wavy margins

Fruit: thin pod, 3–8" (7.5–20 cm) long, opens along 1 side, revealing seeds attached to long tufts of white fuzz

Bloom: spring, summer

Cycle/Origin: perennial; native

Habitat: dry sandy soils, prairies, clearings, and edges of woods and thickets, slopes

Range: far western Texas

Notes: This spreading, branching perennial is a close relative of milkweed, producing a thick white sap in its stems and leaves. The milky sap contains cardiac glycosides, which cause hot flashes, rapid heartbeat, and fatigue. Five thin, sensitive scales in the flower's throat ooze sweet nectar, which attracts flies. A scale turns inward when a fly brushes against it, trapping the insect. When peeled from the stems and dried, the fibrous bark makes strong cords, which were once used by American Indians for fishing and trapping. Orioles prefer to use these same fibers as nest-building material.

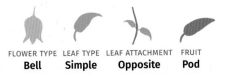

FLOWER TYPE **Bell**   LEAF TYPE **Simple**   LEAF ATTACHMENT **Opposite**   FRUIT **Pod**

73

Mountain Pink

Centaurium beyrichii

Family: Gentian (Gentianaceae)

Height: 6–12" (15–30 cm)

Flower: dense domed cluster on erect densely branched stems; each bright-pink, star-shaped flower, ⅖–¾" (1–2 cm) wide, is made up of 5 pointed, pink petals with white bases fused into a short tube, and has protruding yellow stamens

Leaf: medium green, narrow linear leaves, ⅖–1½" (1–3 cm) long, attached in opposite pairs directly to stems

Fruit: cylindrical capsule, ½" (1.2 cm) long, tapering at both ends, brown at maturity with many dark-brown seeds

Bloom: late spring, summer

Cycle/Origin: annual; native

Habitat: well-drained sand or gravel on rocky limestone or granite hillsides and slopes

Range: north-central to west Texas

Notes: Mountain Pink is best recognized by the perfectly cone-shaped bouquets it forms. Pink petals surround a spiral of yellow anthers that resemble tiny mittens and a bent stigma held apart from the anthers in order to prevent self-pollination. Sometimes called Quinineweed, as pioneers used the dried flowers to treat fevers, but it's probably poisonous to cattle and goats. Only seeds are available for sale, as the plants do not survive transplanting. Sow seeds in the fall.

CLUSTER TYPE	FLOWER TYPE	LEAF TYPE	LEAF ATTACHMENT	FRUIT
Spike	**Regular**	**Simple**	**Opposite**	**Pod**

Tiny Bluet
Houstonia pusilla

Family: Madder (Rubiaceae)

Height: 4–6" (10–15 cm)

Flower: purplish pink-to-blue flowers, ½" (1 cm) wide, have 4 oval pointed petals with a heart-shaped, dark-pink spot at their bases; each delicate-looking flower on a single flower stalk from a leaf attachment

Leaf: oval, fleshy green leaves, ½" (1 cm) long, have edges with fuzzy hairs; leaves are oppositely attached to lower part of reddish-green stem

Bloom: spring

Cycle/Origin: annual; native

Habitat: sandy soils, woodland openings and edges, lawns, rocky outcrops

Range: eastern half of Texas

Notes: Although called a bluet, the color of this wildflower can range from white to pink to blue to purple. There are more than a dozen species of bluet in Texas. Beloved by wildflower enthusiasts because they are such fragile-looking and colorful first blooms of spring. Look for Tiny Bluet in March and April, when daffodils and other spring flowers are blooming in yards. Though a small plant, numerous plants together can cover the ground with a mass of color in shady spots in gardens and lawns.

FLOWER TYPE   LEAF TYPE   LEAF ATTACHMENT
Regular   **Simple**   **Opposite**

Shaggy Purslane
Portulaca pilosa

Family: Purslane (Portulacaceae)

Height: 1–10" (2.5–25 cm)

Flower: single, cup-shaped, rosy pink-to-purple flower, ½" (1 cm) wide, has 5 oblong petals with blunt ends, surrounding a yellow center

Leaf: small, fleshy, narrow leaves, ¾" (2 cm) long, are thick, have pointed tips, and alternate along the reddish-green stems

Bloom: any season, except when very cold in winter

Cycle/Origin: annual, perennial; native

Habitat: dry soils, dunes, rocky outcrops, disturbed sites, along roads and railroads

Range: throughout

Notes: A succulent plant, upright or sprawling, that forms low rounded clumps or flat mats. The leaves vary in shape and color, depending on the climate where it grows, and the amount of hairs on the foliage depends on whether the soil in the area is normally dry or moist. Also called Kiss-me-quick or Pink Purslane. Found throughout the southern United States and from Mexico to South America, where it is a common garden vegetable. Salt tolerant, it grows on beaches along the Gulf of Mexico and the Caribbean, and it has become an invasive weed in warm regions all over the world.

FLOWER TYPE | LEAF TYPE | LEAF ATTACHMENT
Regular | **Simple** | **Alternate**

Carolina Bristlemallow
Modiola caroliniana

Family: Mallow (Malvaceae)

Height: 12–30" (30–76 cm)

Flower: cup-shaped, pink-to-orangish-red flower, ½" (1 cm) wide, has 5 broad fan-shaped petals with darker red lines at bases; yellow, green, and red center; held by green sepals and backed by shorter leaf-like bracts

Leaf: variable broad leaves (can be kidney-shaped, round, or triangular), 2–3" (5–7.5 cm) long; edges toothed or shallowly or deeply divided into 3–7 lobes; on long stalks; sprawling, hairy, many-branched stems

Fruit: round green capsule, turning tan, ½" (1 cm) wide, with segments resembling spokes of a wagon wheel

Bloom: spring, early summer

Cycle/Origin: annual, perennial, biennial; native

Habitat: dry, moist, or salty soils; grasslands, disturbed areas, ditches, lawns, along roads, lakes, and streams

Range: southeastern, south central, extreme southern, and far western Texas

Notes: This creeping wildflower has many branches from the base that root at the nodes wherever they touch the ground. The leaves are poisonous to livestock and avoided by deer and other wildlife. Can be a good ground cover, as it is tolerant of dry conditions and poor soils. Native to the United States only in Texas and the warmer eastern states, but has escaped cultivation and naturalized in the West.

FLOWER TYPE	LEAF TYPE	LEAF ATTACHMENT	FRUIT
Regular	**Simple Lobed**	**Alternate**	**Pod**

Slickseed Fuzzybean
Strophostyles leiosperma

Family: Pea or Bean (Fabaceae)

Height: 24–36" (61–91 cm); vine

Flower: pea-like, pink-to-lavender flowers, ½" (1 cm) wide, each with the upper petal twisted and tipped with dark purple; 1–6 flowers well above leaves on flower stalk, 2–4" (5–10 cm) long

Leaf: fuzzy compound leaves, 2–3" (5–7.5 cm) long, divided into 3 narrowly oval leaflets, 1" (2.5 cm) long; pairs of small lance-shaped leaves (stipules) at the base of each leafstalk

Fruit: green pod, turning dark brown, 1–1½" (2.5–4 cm) long, shaped like a fat string bean and finely haired, contains shiny smooth seeds

Bloom: summer, fall

Cycle/Origin: annual; native

Habitat: dry sandy soils, prairies, open woods, dunes

Range: throughout, except the far western part of Texas

Notes: Common and conspicuous, and aptly named for its smooth dark seeds and hairy, bean-like pods. Strophostyles is from the Greek strophe for "turning" and stulos for "style," referring to the curved flower part, a characteristic of flowers in the genus. Leiosperma means "slick seeds," which are eaten by quail, turkeys, and doves. Often cultivated for its delicate blooms and its ability to quickly cover a trellis. Sometimes called Wild Bean.

FLOWER TYPE	LEAF TYPE	LEAF ATTACHMENT	FRUIT
Irregular	**Compound**	**Alternate**	**Pod**

Spring Beauty
Claytonia virginica

Family: Purslane (Portulacaceae)

Height: 6–10" (15–25 cm)

Flower: star-shaped, white-to-pink flower, ½–¾" (1–2 cm) wide, has 5 pink-veined white petals sometimes spotted with yellow at their bases, around pink-and-white flower parts

Leaf: fleshy, grass-like leaves, 2–4" (5–10 cm) long, are oppositely attached midway up the stem; usually 1 pair of leaves per plant

Bloom: late winter, early spring

Cycle/Origin: perennial; native

Habitat: rich soils, lawns, fields, clearings in woods

Range: eastern third of Texas

Notes: An attractive flower that blooms early in spring, hence its common name. The pink veins on the petals act as runways to guide insects to the nectar. As they "taxi in," the insects load up on pollen by brushing against male flower parts (stamens), then fly to another flower, where they deposit a few grains onto the receptive female flower part (stigma). It often grows in large patches, reproducing from small underground tubers. The potato-like tubers were once gathered for food; as a result, Spring Beauty populations are now reduced. Do not dig up this plant—a variety can be purchased at local garden centers. One of many in the Purslane family, a group of about 600 species of plants worldwide.

FLOWER TYPE   LEAF TYPE   LEAF ATTACHMENT
Regular   **Simple**   **Opposite**

85

Curlytop Smartweed
Polygonum lapathifolium

Family: Buckwheat (Polygonaceae)

Height: 2–6' (0.6–1.8 m)

Flower: upright or nodding slim spike, ½–3" (1–7.5 cm) long, of many tiny, deep-pink or pinkish white-to-white flowers; spike clusters top the stems or grow from the leaf junctions (axis)

Leaf: somewhat limp, oval leaves, 2–12" (5–30 cm) long, are narrow with pointed tips; white glands dot the lower surface and both surfaces often have a dark blotch ("lady's thumb") in the middle; stems are segmented with reddish-green nodes

Bloom: year-round, except in the coldest winter weather

Cycle/Origin: annual; native

Habitat: moist to wet soils, freshwater or brackish mud flats, waste ground, along streams, ponds, and lakes

Range: throughout, except the northeastern corner of Texas

Notes: An outstanding food plant for wildlife. The seeds of this abundant buckwheat are eaten by a wide variety of game birds, waterfowl, muskrats, raccoons, squirrels, and mice. Found throughout the US, Canada, and north into the Arctic. "Smartweed" refers to the sharp burning sensation the leaves impart when eaten. The leaves were once made into a tea to treat fevers and constipation. Commonly thought to be native to Texas, but some botanists believe that this willowy, common weed was actually introduced from Eurasia.

CLUSTER TYPE	FLOWER TYPE	LEAF TYPE	LEAF ATTACHMENT
Spike	**Regular**	**Simple**	**Alternate**

Rose Palafox
Palafoxia rosea

Family: Aster (Asteraceae)

Height: 12–24" (30–61 cm)

Flower: frilly, round, pink-to-lavender flower heads, ⅝" (1.5 cm) wide, each with 12–25 densely packed, tiny disk flowers (florets) and protruding maroon flower parts; loose groups of flower heads; each head on its own leafless flower stalk

Leaf: slender oval leaves, 1–3" (2.5–7.5 cm) long, with pointed tips and covered with short, fuzzy white hairs; alternate, but pairs of leaves widely spaced from the next pair; additional smaller leaves at each leaf junction

Bloom: summer, fall

Cycle/Origin: annual; native

Habitat: sandy soils, deserts, along roads, prairies, slopes

Range: throughout, except the far western part of Texas

Notes: An upright, delicate-looking annual with stiff wiry stems and widely spaced leaves. Lacking ray flowers, the flower heads appear shaggy due to the maroon flower parts protruding from the tubular florets. Blossoms attract butterflies, bees, and beetles. Used in folk medicine for the treatment of fever, chills, and nausea. Easily cultivated from seed. Related to Sand Palafox (pg. 113), which has larger flower heads that have both ray and disk flowers.

FLOWER TYPE **Composite** LEAF TYPE **Simple** LEAF ATTACHMENT **Alternate**

Drummond Wood Sorrel

Oxalis drummondii

Family: Wood Sorrel (Oxalidaceae)

Height: 6–12" (15–30 cm)

Flower: pink flowers, ¾" (2 cm) wide, with yellow throats; each blossom has 5 broad, separated, outward-curving petals with white bases, a white-and-yellow center, and is on a long, leafless, reddish-green flower stalk

Leaf: clover-like basal leaves, 1–2" (2.5–5 cm) wide, green (sometimes purple-splotched), divided into 3 heart-shaped leaflets; each leaflet is attached at the tip of the heart to a long leafstalk; leaflets fold in cloudy weather and at night, looking like a closed umbrella

Bloom: summer

Cycle/Origin: perennial; native

Habitat: sandy or rocky limestone soils, prairies, lawns

Range: central, southern, and western Texas

Notes: The showiest of a dozen species of wood sorrel in Texas. Foliage of plants in the genus Oxalis (Greek for "sour") contains oxalic acid, which is secreted as sharp calcium oxalate crystals. The leaves, stems, and seedpods of this plant have a sour taste. The tart leaves have been used in salads, but the crystals are hard on the kidneys, and consuming a lot of the foliage should be avoided. Montezuma Quail, which have clown-like faces and are an endangered species in Texas, dig up and eat wood sorrel bulbs.

FLOWER TYPE
Regular

LEAF TYPE
Compound

LEAF ATTACHMENT
Basal

fruit

Trailing Ratany
Krameria lanceolata

Family: Ratany (Krameriaceae)

Height: 2–5' (61–152 cm)

Flower: oddly shaped, purplish-pink flowers, ¾" (2 cm) wide, each with 5 pointed pink petal-like sepals that are unequal in size around 5 tiny magenta-and-green petals (3 upper petals are fused into a claw); each flower arises between a pair of hairy green bracts

Leaf: fuzzy, narrow, whitish-green leaves, 1" (2.5 cm) long, have spiny edges; attached along woody stems

Fruit: fuzzy, round green pod, ½" (1 cm) wide, turning brown, with short spines that have minute barbs

Bloom: spring, summer, fall

Cycle/Origin: perennial; native

Habitat: prairies, open woods, cliffs, rocky slopes and ridges, among grasses

Range: throughout, except the far eastern edge of Texas

Notes: Trailing Ratany is a multi-branched, sprawling plant that spreads from a woody base and has unusual-looking flowers. All species in the genus Krameria obtain part of their nutrients through the roots of nearby plants (semiparasitic). Instead of producing nectar, the flowers attract insect pollinators by secreting oil, which is collected by bees and mixed with pollen to make food for their larvae. Although not abundant, it is found throughout the state, except in the moist pine forests of eastern Texas.

FLOWER TYPE	LEAF TYPE	LEAF ATTACHMENT	FRUIT
Irregular	**Simple**	**Alternate**	**Pod**

Nuttall Sensitive Briar

Mimosa nuttallii

Family: Pea or Bean (Fabaceae)

Height: 3–4' (.9–1.2 m); vine

Flower: bright-pink, round cluster, ¾–1" (2–2.5 cm) wide, of many tiny tubular flowers; flower parts supporting pollen rise above tubules, appearing like yellow dots floating in the air; each cluster grows singly on stalk

Leaf: twice compound leaves, 2–6" (5–15 cm) long, divided into 4–8 pairs of oblong leaflets and again into 8–15 pairs of tiny subleaflets; thorny leafstalks

Fruit: long, slim, ribbed green pod, 1–5" (2.5–13 cm) long, turning brown, has edges covered with thorns

Bloom: spring, summer

Cycle/Origin: perennial; native

Habitat: disturbed areas, woodland openings, prairies

Range: northern and eastern Texas

Notes: The ball-shaped pink flower heads resemble firework explosions in miniature. "Sensitive" refers to the response to touch of the tiny subleaflets–they fold together for 4–5 minutes after being lightly touched. All subleaflets close even when only one nearby is tapped. Plant behavior usually doesn't occur quickly enough for us to detect the motion, but one is able to do so with this plant. This action protects the foliage, presenting thorns on the leafstalks to any grazing deer or rabbits. Also aptly called Cat's Claw because of the shape of the thorns on the sprawling or trailing stems.

CLUSTER TYPE	FLOWER TYPE	LEAF TYPE	LEAF ATTACHMENT	FRUIT
Round	**Tube**	**Twice Compound**	**Alternate**	**Pod**

Prairie Rose Gentian

Sabatia campestris

Family: Gentian (Gentianaceae)

Height: 6–20" (15–50 cm)

Flower: star-shaped, dark-pink (rarely white) flower, 1" (2.5 cm) wide, has 5 wedge-shaped petals with white bases; bright yellow-and-green center with twisted flower parts (stamens) is also shaped like a star

Leaf: widely spaced pairs of oval leaves, ½–1" (1–2.5 cm) long, have wide bases clasping the stem; each pair of leaves rotated at right angles to next pair

Bloom: spring, summer

Cycle/Origin: annual; native

Habitat: rich acidic soils, prairies, rocky woods, meadows, stream banks, roadsides, abandoned fields, sun

Range: eastern half of Texas

Notes: Also called Texas Star for the shape of the blooms, this is one of eight pink-flowered gentians in the state. "Prairie" in the common name is for the habitat where it is frequently found. Native to the south-central United States, from Texas east to Mississippi and north to Iowa and Illinois. Prairie Rose Gentian is underused as a cultivated garden plant. Its pleasantly fragrant bloom makes a good cut flower, but please don't pick it from the wild.

FLOWER TYPE
Regular

LEAF TYPE
Simple

LEAF ATTACHMENT
Opposite

LEAF ATTACHMENT
Clasping

Prairie False Foxglove
Agalinis heterophylla

Family: Snapdragon (Scrophulariaceae)

Height: 12–36" (30–91 cm)

Flower: trumpet-shaped, pink-to-purple flower, 1" (2.5 cm) long, with 5 lobed, fuzzy-edged petals flaring widely at the mouth and dark rose-pink spots dotting the white throat; pairs of flowers on short stalks line the top of stem

Leaf: narrow, light-green leaves, 1–3" (2.5–7.5 cm) long; lower leaves lobed, upper leaves have smooth edges and are smaller toward top of square stem; single or branching stems: leaves are often purple

Fruit: round green pod, turning brown, ¼" (.6 cm) wide

Bloom: summer, fall

Cycle/Origin: annual; native

Habitat: moist sandy soils, prairies, disturbed areas

Range: eastern half of Texas

Notes: One of only 17 species of false foxglove in Texas, this wildflower is difficult to distinguish from other false foxgloves with pink or purple flowers. Derives some of its nutrients by inserting its roots into the roots of other plants (semiparasitic). Common Buckeye caterpillars eat the leaves, making the plant a good choice for butterfly gardens. Upper leaves are simple, but the lower leaves are lobed and often fall off by the time the plant flowers.

FLOWER TYPE
Tube

LEAF TYPE
Simple

LEAF TYPE
Simple Lobed

LEAF ATTACHMENT
Opposite

FRUIT
Pod

Black Prairie Clover

Dalea frutescens

Family: Pea or Bean (Fabaceae)

Height: 8–36" (20–91 cm); shrub

Flower: short spike cluster, 1" (2.5 cm) long, of 5–25 small, pea-like, magenta-and-cream flowers; largest petal is cream-colored

Leaf: fine fern-like leaves, 1" (2.5 cm) long, are made up of about 8 pairs of tiny narrow leaflets dotted with glands on their lower surfaces; leaves on short stalks

Bloom: summer, fall

Cycle/Origin: perennial; native

Habitat: dry, rocky limestone hillsides with shallow soils

Range: central and western Texas

Notes: This fast-growing, low-mounding shrub has finely textured green foliage covered with short spikes of attractive pink-and-cream flowers. Genus name Dalea honors English botanist Samuel Dale, and species name frutescens refers to its shrubby form. Similar to the closely related Feather Plume (pg. 107), but its blossoms lack the hairy sepals of that species. Drought-resistant, Black Prairie Clover requires little maintenance when used in informal hedges or as ground cover. In the United States, found mostly in Texas and limited portions of New Mexico and Oklahoma. Also ranges farther south into Chihuahua, Coahuila, and Nuevo León, northern states in Mexico.

CLUSTER TYPE
Spike

FLOWER TYPE
Irregular

LEAF TYPE
Compound

LEAF ATTACHMENT
Alternate

Autumn Sage
Salvia greggii

Family: Mint (Lamiaceae)

Height: 24–36" (30-122 cm)

Flower: short, tight spikes of two-lipped, bright-red or deep-pink, tubular flowers, 1" (2.5 cm) long, blooming on stems 3–6" above the leaves. Blooms can also be yellow, white, purple, or any shade of these colors

Leaf: evergreen, oval, smooth-edged leaves, 1–2" (2.5–5 cm) long, with rounded tips, attach on thin stalks opposite each other. New stalks and smaller leaves originate at base of the stems of each pair of larger leaves forming dense whorls of leaves that are widely spaced on square stems from the other leaf whorls. Stems can be woody and are brittle.

Fruit: cup-shaped, papery beige capsule ½" (1 cm) long, holds 4 tiny seeds

Bloom: spring, summer, fall

Cycle/Origin: perennial; native

Habitat: rocky slopes, well-drained soils

Range: central, south-central, and west Texas

Notes: Cultivated throughout the Southwest, this low-mounding shrub is treasured for its drought tolerance, resistance to being eaten by deer and rabbits, and persistent blooming spring through fall, which attracts butterflies and hummingbirds. The leaves are aromatic, and the flowers are edible. A gorgeous plant, it readily reseeds in moist soil.

CLUSTER TYPE
Spike

FLOWER TYPE
Tube

LEAF TYPE
Simple

LEAF ATTACHMENT
Opposite

LEAF ATTACHMENT
Whorl

FRUIT
Pod

Spotted Bee Balm
Monarda punctata

Family: Mint (Lamiaceae)

Height: 12–36" (30–91 cm)

Flower: ragged spike cluster, 1–2" (2.5–5 cm) wide, made up of dense whorls of downward-curving, prominent, pink-to-purple or white-and-green bracts (often mistaken for petals), alternating with maroon-spotted yellow flowers; each tubular flower, 1" (2.5 cm) long, has 2 petals (lips); 2–5 whorls along the upper stem

Leaf: lance-shaped leaves, 1–3" (2.5–7.5 cm) long, with toothed or smooth edges; hairy, grayish-green stems

Bloom: spring, summer

Cycle/Origin: annual, perennial, biennial; native

Habitat: dry, sandy soils; old fields, dunes, rocky woodlands

Range: throughout

Notes: Plants in the Mint family can be identified by their square stems and oppositely attached leaves. In addition, the stems and leaves of most plants in the family are scented. Spotted Bee Balm is also known as Chinese Pagoda for the unique arrangement of the flowers and bracts. Sometimes called Dotted Horsemint, American Indians used it to treat fevers and colds or hung it up to dry, perfuming a lodge with its minty fragrance. Not grazed upon by wildlife, this wildflower can cover extensive areas in the wild. Often cultivated in gardens, its nectar attracts hummingbirds.

CLUSTER TYPE	FLOWER TYPE	LEAF TYPE	LEAF ATTACHMENT
Spike	**Irregular**	**Simple**	**Opposite**

Feather Plume
Dalea formosa

Family: Pea or Bean (Fabaceae)

Height: 18–36" (45–91 cm); shrub

Flower: short magenta-and-yellow spike cluster, 1–2" (2.5–5 cm) long, composed of 2–9 small pea-like magenta flowers with the largest petal cream or yellow, surrounded by feathery sepals

Leaf: feather-like, grayish-green leaves, ¼–½" (.6–1 cm) long, made up of 7–15 tiny narrow leaflets; leaves are semi-evergreen

Bloom: spring, summer, fall; especially after rainfall

Cycle/Origin: perennial; native

Habitat: deserts, prairies, rocky hillsides, mountainsides

Range: western half of Texas

Notes: Sometimes called Feather Dalea, this hardy, low-growing shrub is a good choice for cultivation in the Southwest. It tolerates cold and heat, and it blooms profusely with little water. Don't overwater—the plant will become leggy. Pollinated by bees, but butterflies also visit the blossoms. One of more than 30 species of prairie clover in Texas. Feather Plume is especially common in the Chihuahuan Desert, part of which is located in southwestern Texas, but the plant is also found in New Mexico, Arizona, Colorado, Utah, and northern Mexico.

CLUSTER TYPE	FLOWER TYPE	LEAF TYPE	LEAF ATTACHMENT
Spike	**Irregular**	**Compound**	**Alternate**

fruit

Everlasting Pea
Lathyrus latifolius

Family: Pea or Bean (Fabaceae)

Height: 3–7' (.9–2.1 m); vine

Flower: loose spike cluster, 1–5" (2.5–13 cm) long, of 4–10 pea-like pink flowers; each blossom, 1" (2.5 cm) wide, is on a long stem

Leaf: compound leaves, 4" (10 cm) long, of 2 lance-shaped or elliptical leaflets; each leaflet, 1–3" (2.5–7.5 cm) long, at end of a flat winged stalk; may have forked thread-like projection (tendril) from the tip of leafstalk; multiple stems with many branches

Fruit: slender bean-like green pod, turning yellow, 2½–4" (6–10 cm) long, contains 10–15 cylindrical poisonous black seeds

Bloom: summer, fall

Cycle/Origin: perennial; nonnative

Habitat: disturbed soils, roadsides, fields, waste areas

Range: throughout

Notes: This introduced plant is very invasive, readily escaping from cultivation or overrunning a garden. A weak-stemmed vine that climbs on other plants by taking hold with its forked tendrils. Has two pair of narrow, pointed appendages (stipules) at the base of each leafstalk. Stems and leafstalks are winged. However, the flower stalk lacks wings and can be as long as 8 inches (20 cm). Flowers are usually pink, but can be pink and white or blue to white.

CLUSTER TYPE	FLOWER TYPE	LEAF TYPE	LEAF ATTACHMENT	FRUIT
Spike	**Irregular**	**Compound**	**Alternate**	**Pod**

Texas Rock Rose
Pavonia lasiopetala

Family: Mallow (Malvaceae)

Height: 12–24" (30–61 cm); shrub

Flower: hibiscus-like, pink-to-rose flowers, 1½" (4 cm) wide, have 5 broad fan-shaped petals surrounding protruding pink-and-yellow flower parts; each blossom on a slim flower stalk from leaf junctions

Leaf: heart-shaped, dark-green leaves, 1–3" (2.5–7.5 cm) long, are fuzzy, stalked, and have toothed margins; leaves alternate along hairy, red stems

Bloom: spring, summer, fall

Cycle/Origin: perennial; native

Habitat: dry, rocky limestone soils; open woods, thickets

Range: southern and far western Texas, especially along the Rio Grande

Notes: An upright small shrub with a single branching red stem and leaves covered with hairs. Fused flower parts (stamens) form a column in the center on the flower. Found in the wild only in a limited area of Texas and in Mexico, but is a popular accent plant of gardeners. Tolerates full sun to a half day of shade, and the blooms open in the morning and close by midafternoon. Also called Texas Swampmallow, but this wildflower is drought-tolerant and frequently found growing in dry soil.

FLOWER TYPE
Regular

LEAF TYPE
Simple

LEAF ATTACHMENT
Alternate

Sand Palafox
Palafoxia hookeriana

Family: Aster (Asteraceae)

Height: 2–4' (61–122 cm)

Flower: large pink flower heads, 1½" (4 cm) wide, each with 8–13 petals (ray flowers) with 3 narrow lobes; petals ring a mounded center of upright disk flowers with protruding maroon flower parts; loose groups of flower heads at the top of stem; each head on its own flower stalk

Leaf: lance-shaped leaves, 2–4" (5–10 cm) long, are long and slim, sticky, have pointed tips and short, fuzzy, white hairs lining the edges; purplish-brown stem

Bloom: summer, fall

Cycle/Origin: annual; native

Habitat: sandy soils, prairies, disturbed sites, fields

Range: far southern, southeastern, south-central, and coastal Texas

Notes: This striking wildflower is often cultivated in Texas gardens since it blooms profusely throughout the summer and fall. The ray flowers are so deeply lobed that the flower heads appear to have three times the number of their actual petals. In the United States, it grows in the wild only in the southern region of Texas on the Sand Plains, where the subtropical climate has hot, humid summers and mild winters. The Sand Plains is a 2–million-acre (800,000 ha) layer of sand blown inland in the last 12,000 years from the Gulf of Mexico.

FLOWER TYPE **Composite**   LEAF TYPE **Simple**   LEAF ATTACHMENT **Alternate**

Texas Thistle
Cirsium texanum

Family: Aster (Asteraceae)

Height: 2–5' (61–152 cm)

Flower: purplish-pink flower head, 1½" (4 cm) wide, made up of thin, tubular disk flowers; sits on a prickly green base; 1 to several flower heads per stem

Leaf: dark-green leaves, 4–12" (10–30 cm) long, are narrow, elliptical, and divided into 3–9 triangular lobes, each ending in a sharp spine; white hairs on stems and undersides of leaves; basal leaves are large, upper leaves are smaller

Bloom: spring, summer

Cycle/Origin: biennial; native

Habitat: dry disturbed soils, prairies, open fields, roadsides, along railroads

Range: throughout, but especially southern, central, and western Texas

Notes: Texas Thistle is a true biennial, producing a rosette of leaves its first year and sending up a tall flower stalk in the second. A preferred flower of large bees and butterflies, its little seeds are attached to tiny parachute-like thistledown that carry them away on the wind after pollination. The seeds are a favorite food of the Lesser Goldfinch, which raises its young in late summer. This bird lines its nest with the thistledown produced after the thistles flower.

FLOWER TYPE
Composite

LEAF TYPE
Simple Lobed

LEAF ATTACHMENT
Alternate

LEAF ATTACHMENT
Clasping

LEAF ATTACHMENT
Basal

Lemon Bee Balm
Monarda citriodora

Family: Mint (Lamiaceae)

Height: 24–32" (61–80 cm)

Flower: cylindrical, purplish-pink spike cluster, 1½" (4 cm) wide, made up of layered whorls of many flowers; each flower, ½" (1 cm) long, has 2 petals (lips); hood-shaped hairy upper lip is smaller than 3–lobed, ragged-tipped lower lip with pink spots; hairy, purplish-pink bracts below each flower whorl

Leaf: lemon-scented, oval, bright-green leaves, 1–2½" (2.5–6 cm) long, with coarse-toothed edges and pointed tips; fuzzy square stem

Bloom: spring, summer, fall

Cycle/Origin: annual, perennial, biennial; native

Habitat: tallgrass prairies, rangelands, meadows, open woodlands, roadsides, sun

Range: throughout

Notes: Species name citriodora, derived from the Latin words for "citrus" and "odor," refers to the strong, lemony fragrance emitted by the leaves, flowers, and stems. Citronella in the candles often used in backyards to repel insects comes from the oil of this plant. Younger leaves and petals are dried and included in herbal tea mixtures. Hopi Indians once used the leaves in cooking to flavor wild game. Occurs in large stands in the wild. Bees and butterflies are drawn to the flowers, so this plant is frequently cultivated.

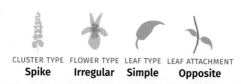

CLUSTER TYPE **Spike**   FLOWER TYPE **Irregular**   LEAF TYPE **Simple**   LEAF ATTACHMENT **Opposite**

Texas Skeleton Plant

Lygodesmia texana

Family: Aster (Asteraceae)

Height: 10–24" (25–61 cm)

Flower: pink or lavender flower heads, 1½–2" (4–5 cm) wide, have 11 narrow, pink ray flowers (no disk flowers) with white bases and fringed tips, around protruding white and pinkish-purple flower parts; single blossom atop each leafless flower stalk

Leaf: few narrow basal leaves, 4–8" (10–20 cm) long, that wilt by the time the plant flowers; leaves are divided into irregular thread-like lobes; tiny scale-like upper leaves on smooth, nearly leafless stems

Bloom: any season, except in the coldest winter weather

Cycle/Origin: perennial; native

Habitat: dry limestone or red sandy soils, oak-juniper woodlands, prairies, mesquite brushlands, rocky slopes

Range: throughout, except eastern Texas

Notes: This clumping aster starts as a basal rosette of straw-like leaves, thus another common name, Flowering Straw. Has rarely branching and nearly leafless stems when blooming. "Skeleton" is for the lack of leaves on the green stems. Also called Milk Pink for the milky sap in the hollow stems. The fragile-looking blossoms open for only a few hours in the morning, but are popular with butterflies seeking nectar. In the United States, found only in Texas and limited areas of Oklahoma and New Mexico. Also occurs in Mexico.

FLOWER TYPE **Composite** LEAF TYPE **Simple** LEAF TYPE **Simple Lobed** LEAF ATTACHMENT **Basal**

119

Wine Cup
Callirhoe involucrata

Family: Mallow (Malvaceae)

Height: 12–24" (30–61 cm)

Flower: cup-shaped, rose pink-to-purplish-red flowers, 1½–2½" (4–6 cm) wide, consist of 5 oblong petals with white bases and blunt tips, surrounding pale-yellow flower parts

Leaf: fan-shaped leaves, 1–2" (2.5–5 cm) wide, are deeply divided into thin or broad, ragged lobes; alternately attached to trailing stems

Bloom: spring, summer

Cycle/Origin: perennial; native

Habitat: prairies, open woods, thickets, disturbed areas

Range: throughout Texas, except the far western part of the state

Notes: Named for the shape and color of the blooms. The flowers dry to a purple color, thus it is also known as Purple Poppy Mallow. This is a sprawling plant that forms low mats of vegetation with the flowers rising above on hairy, thin stalks. Flowers are pollinated mainly by bees and other insects. As a cure for the common cold, Plains Indians inhaled the smoke produced by burning the edible dried root.

FLOWER TYPE
Regular

LEAF TYPE
Simple Lobed

LEAF ATTACHMENT
Alternate

Virginia Tephrosia
Tephrosia virginiana

Family: Pea or Bean (Fabaceae)

Height: 12–24" (30–61 cm)

Flower: compact spike cluster, 1½–3" (4–7.5 cm) long, of small pink-and-white, pea-like flowers; each flower has a larger white or cream upper petal (standard), pink wings, and lower rose-pink petals (keel)

Leaf: compound feather-like leaves, 7" (18 cm) long, made up of 5–12 pairs of hairy, elliptical leaflets, 1" (2.5 cm) long, and 1 end (terminal) leaflet; leaves alternate on multiple stems with long hairs

Fruit: hairy green pod, turning brown to black, 2" (5 cm) long, is pea-like and flattened lengthwise

Bloom: spring, summer

Cycle/Origin: perennial; native

Habitat: dry, sandy acidic soils; thickets, open pinewoods

Range: scattered throughout northern, eastern, and central Texas

Notes: Tephros is Greek for "hoary," for the grayish cast produced by the silky hairs on the leaves and stems. Wildlife and livestock avoid the poisonous leaves, thus another common name, Goat's Rue. Southern Cloudywing butterfly caterpillars depend on this plant for food, despite the leaves containing rotenone, a chemical used as an insecticide. American Indians put the leaves in streams to stun fish, scooping them up when they floated to the surface.

CLUSTER TYPE
Spike

FLOWER TYPE
Irregular

LEAF TYPE
Compound

LEAF ATTACHMENT
Alternate

FRUIT
Pod

fruit

Ram's Horn
Proboscidea louisianica

Family: Sesame (Pedaliaceae)

Height: 12–36" (30–91 cm)

Flower: trumpet-shaped flower, 2" (5 cm) long, is pale-to-dark pink and has 5 fused petals flaring into 2 upper and 3 lower lobes, with a yellow line and violet splotches in the throat

Leaf: fuzzy, nearly round leaves, 2–6" (5–15 cm) wide, are wrinkled with wavy or shallowly lobed edges and on long stalks; hairy, sticky, reddish-green branches

Fruit: fuzzy curved okra-like pod, 7" (18 cm) long, dries and splits lengthwise into 2 curving sharp "claws"

Bloom: spring, summer, fall

Cycle/Origin: annual; native

Habitat: dry, sandy, or clay soils; disturbed sites, pastures, roadsides, along washes, slopes

Range: throughout, except the far eastern part of Texas

Notes: Named for the split curved dry pods that resemble curved horns. Also known as Devil's Claw. The pods catch on the legs of passing animals or on the heels of hikers, dispersing the seeds. American Indians of the Southwest grow this plant for the fibers of the dry pods, using them in basketry. Young pods are cooked as one would prepare okra. The flowers and pods are often hidden below an umbrella of broad leaves. The yellow stripe in the flower's throat guides bees to the nectar.

FLOWER TYPE
Tube

LEAF TYPE
Simple

LEAF TYPE
Simple Lobed

LEAF ATTACHMENT
Opposite

FRUIT
Pod

Showy Evening Primrose
Oenothera speciosa

Family: Evening primrose (Onagraceae)

Height: 8–24" (20–61 cm)

Flower: shallow bowl-shaped pink flower, 2–3" (5–7.5 cm) wide, has 4 pink-veined petals that are broadly heart-shaped and shallowly notched on outer edges; yellow center ringed with white; solitary flower attaches at each upper leaf junction

Leaf: lance-shaped or oval leaves, 1–3" (2.5–7.5 cm) long, with edges either smooth, shallowly toothed, or deeply cleft into pointed lobes; multiple stems

Fruit: slim green pod, turning brown, ½–1" (1–2.5 cm) long, club-shaped, 4–sided, lengthwise grooves

Bloom: spring, summer

Cycle/Origin: perennial; nonnative

Habitat: dry disturbed soils, prairies, roadsides, open woods, fallow fields

Range: throughout

Notes: Also called Pinkladies for the delicate-looking, shell-pink flowers. Despite its fragile appearance, the plant is fairly heat and drought-tolerant. Although in the Evening primrose family, the flowers are open only in daylight and pollinated by day-flying insects. Originating in Mexico and the Southwest, this pretty bloom is widely cultivated and has naturalized over much of the southern half of the United States. Spreads by creeping roots; can overtake gardens.

FLOWER TYPE	LEAF TYPE	LEAF TYPE	LEAF ATTACHMENT	FRUIT
Regular	**Simple**	**Simple Lobed**	**Alternate**	**Pod**

Downy Phlox
Phlox pilosa

Family: Phlox (Polemoniaceae)

Height: 10–24" (25–61 cm)

Flower: fragrant flat cluster, 2–3" (5–7.5 cm) wide, of pink-to-lavender flowers; each blossom, 1" (2.5 cm) wide, is made up of 5 broad, wedge-shaped petals fused into a short tube at the base

Leaf: narrow or broad leaves, 1–5" (2.5–13 cm) long, have hairy edges, pointed tips, and are rounded at the base; leaves grow in opposite pairs along the white-haired stem

Bloom: early spring, summer; sometimes blooms again in early fall

Cycle/Origin: perennial; native

Habitat: open woods, along roads, on fences, dry hillsides, in prairies

Range: eastern and central Texas

Notes: Downy Phlox is a single- or multi-stemmed wildflower that is often found growing in woodland edges or openings along country roads. Quite variable in form (its flowers are occasionally white), but its leaves and stems are always covered with stiff white hairs, thus the species name pilosa, meaning "hairy." The closed flower buds have twisted petals appearing like a torch, giving rise to the genus name Phlox, Greek for "flame." Closely related to the familiar garden phlox. Ranges over the entire eastern half of the United States and Canada.

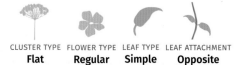

CLUSTER TYPE	FLOWER TYPE	LEAF TYPE	LEAF ATTACHMENT
Flat	**Regular**	**Simple**	**Opposite**

Henbit Deadnettle

Lamium amplexicaule

Family: Mint (Lamiaceae)

Height: 6–16" (15–40 cm)

Flower: round cluster, 2–3" (5–7.5 cm) wide, of 4–5 pink-to-purple flowers; each flower, 1" (2.5 cm) long, has 1 dark-pink, hairy, protruding upper lobe and 2 light-pink lower lobes with dark-rose spots

Leaf: rounded or fan-shaped leaves, 1" (2.5 cm) wide, are green with purple edges and have 5 bluntly toothed lobes and very wrinkled upper surfaces; upper leaves are stalkless, attaching just below flowers; lower leaves are stalked; square, hollow, green stem has with purplish base

Bloom: early spring, summer

Cycle/Origin: annual, biennial; nonnative

Habitat: dry disturbed soils, old fields, lawns, parks

Range: throughout

Notes: Like others in the Mint family, Henbit Deadnettle flowers look somewhat like tiny orchids. Unlike other mints, its leaves and stems do not have the characteristic minty fragrance when crushed. Introduced from Europe and the Mediterranean region to the southern states for erosion control, this short plant has become an invasive weed throughout the US. Can grow plantlets from pieces of the stem, thus when it is tilled under with the soil, it often forms large populations that cover entire fields with a pink carpet of flowers.

CLUSTER TYPE
Round

FLOWER TYPE
Irregular

LEAF TYPE
Simple Lobed

LEAF ATTACHMENT
Opposite

Annual Phlox
Phlox drummondii

Family: Phlox (Polemoniaceae)

Height: 4–20" (10–50 cm)

Flower: loose, flat cluster, 2–6" (5–15 cm) wide, of dark-pink (usually), white, or red flowers; each blossom, 1" (2.5 cm) wide, made of 5 blunt-tipped overlapping petals around a contrasting center; petals fuse at base to form a long, narrow tube; clusters sit high above leaves atop hairy, sticky stem

Leaf: oblong leaves, 2–4" (5–10 cm) long; lower leaves are oppositely attached, upper leaves alternate on stem that has many glandular hairs

Bloom: early spring, summer

Cycle/Origin: annual; native

Habitat: dry to moist sandy soils, roadsides, disturbed areas, old fields, woodland clearings

Range: eastern two-thirds of Texas

Notes: Native to central and eastern Texas, Annual Phlox is also widely cultivated and has escaped and naturalized in the sandy soils of disturbed areas. The flowers of cultivated varieties are lavender, lime green, magenta, pink, yellow, white, or red (see inset), and escaped plants with these colors can be found near old gardens or abandoned houses. This is a fragrant flower that likes cool spring weather and does best at temperatures below 85° F (29°C).

CLUSTER TYPE
Flat

FLOWER TYPE
Regular

LEAF TYPE
Simple

LEAF ATTACHMENT
Alternate

LEAF ATTACHMENT
Opposite

Showy False Dragonhead
Physostegia pulchella

Family: Mint (Lamiaceae)

Height: 1–5' (30–152 cm)

Flower: dense spike cluster, 2–6" (5–15 cm) long, of many pink or lavender flowers; each flower, 1" (2.5 cm) long, made up of wrinkled petals fused to form tube with 2 flaring petals (lips); 3-lobed lower lip has purplish-pink spots and stripes; throat opening is nearly rectangular

Leaf: slender, pointed, oval leaves, 1–5" (2.5–13 cm) long, often with sharply toothed edges; lower leaves on long stalks, smaller upper leaves stalkless; smooth 4-angled hollow stem

Bloom: spring, early summer

Cycle/Origin: perennial; native

Habitat: moist to wet soils, prairies, bottomlands, stream banks, marshes, seepages, ditches, along highways

Range: eastern Texas

Notes: The wildflowers in the Physostegia genus are sometimes called Obedient Plants for the flowers, which remain in whatever position they are placed. A member of the Mint family, often one of the most common plant families found in prairies. The showy flower spike blooms from the bottom up, and new flowers continue to open even after it is cut. Often planted in wildflower gardens. Showy False Dragonhead is native only to Texas.

CLUSTER TYPE
Spike

FLOWER TYPE
Irregular

LEAF TYPE
Simple

LEAF ATTACHMENT
Opposite

LEAF ATTACHMENT
Clasping

Scarlet Beeblossom
Oenothera suffrutescens

Family: Evening primrose (Onagraceae)

Height: 8–24" (20–61 cm)

Flower: spike cluster, 2–16" (5–40 cm) long, of flowers that turn overnight from white to pink to red; each blossom has 4 clawed petals and dangling red-tipped white flower parts (anthers) backed by 4 downward-curving, pointed, pinkish-green sepals

Leaf: narrow, lance-shaped, grayish-green leaves, ½–3" (1–7.5 cm) long, are stalkless with pointed tips and have irregularly toothed or smooth edges; upper leaves smaller; several stems branching from base

Fruit: wrinkled diamond-shaped fruit, ½" (1 cm) long

Bloom: spring, summer, fall

Cycle/Origin: perennial; native

Habitat: sandy soils, in disturbed areas, old fields, prairies, plains, sun

Range: western half of Texas

Notes: This pretty, airy flower starts out nearly white in the evening when it first opens, attracting moths that pollinate it that night. Turns pink by morning and red by afternoon, thus "Scarlet" in the common name. Flowers at bottom of spike open first. Spreads by underground stems (rhizomes), forming masses of plants. Can colonize in heavily grazed or disturbed sites outside of its natural range. American Indians drank tea made from it to treat upset stomachs.

CLUSTER TYPE **Spike**   FLOWER TYPE **Irregular**   LEAF TYPE **Simple**   LEAF ATTACHMENT **Alternate**   FRUIT **Pod**

Tievine
Ipomoea cordatotriloba

Family: Morning Glory (Convolvulaceae)

Height: 12–15' (3.7–4.6 m); vine

Flower: trumpet-shaped flowers, 2¼" (5.5 cm) wide, made up of fused, purplish-pink petals with darker pink bases, and flaring widely at the mouth; 1 to several blooms per short stalk arising from leaf junction

Leaf: variable leaves, 1–4" (2.5–10 cm) long, can be heart-shaped, divided into 3–5 lobes or lacking lobes; on long stalks alternating along the twining stem

Bloom: spring, summer, fall

Cycle/Origin: perennial; native

Habitat: disturbed soils, old fields, thickets, along streams, woodland edges

Range: southern, central, and eastern Texas; ranging over half of the state

Notes: The species name cordatotriloba is from two Latin words meaning "heart" and "three-lobed," referring to the fact that leaves on the same plant vary from heart-shaped to lobed. However, the leaves can also have smooth edges with no lobes at all. Found throughout the Southeast, where it is sometimes called Cotton Morning Glory for its unfortunate weedy habit of invading cotton fields. The vines trail along the ground or twine in shrubs a few feet high. Spectacular blooms open in early morning and wilt by afternoon, thus the family name, Morning Glory.

FLOWER TYPE
Tube

LEAF TYPE
Simple Lobed

LEAF ATTACHMENT
Alternate

fruit

Rouge Plant
Rivina humilis

Family: Pokeweed (Phytolaccaceae)

Height: 1–5' (30–152 cm)

Flower: upright or drooping spike cluster, 3–6" (7.5–15 cm) long, with many tiny pink or white flowers; each flower, ¼" (.6 cm) wide, has 4 petal-like sepals but lacks petals; blooms from bottom of spike upward

Leaf: broad, lance-shaped, bright-green leaves, 1–6" (2.5–15 cm) long, are smooth with wavy edges, have pointed tips and rounded bases, and are on stalks

Fruit: green berry, turning glossy and bright red, ½" (1 cm) wide; in drooping or upright clusters on green (turning red) stems

Bloom: year-round, except in the coldest winter weather

Cycle/Origin: perennial; native

Habitat: chaparral, rocky slopes, along streams

Range: throughout, except the northwestern part of Texas

Notes: A short, upright or trailing, bushy plant usually found in small colonies in shady locations. Also called Pigeonberry. Although toxic to humans, birds find the berries irresistible and will flock to gardens where the plant is grown. Crushing the ripe berries yields a red dye that has been used as ink or to color cloth. In Mexico, the leaves were historically used to treat open wounds. Leaf extracts of this plant are weakly effective against some infectious bacteria. Native to the southern United States and south through South America.

CLUSTER TYPE
Spike

FLOWER TYPE
Regular

LEAF TYPE
Simple

LEAF ATTACHMENT
Alternate

FRUIT
Berry

Sweetscent Camphorweed
Pluchea odorata

Family: Aster (Asteraceae)

Height: 8–32" (20–80 cm)

Flower: dark-or light-pink flat cluster, 3–6" (7.5–15 cm) wide, of densely packed, tiny flower heads; each flower head, ¼–½" (.6–1 cm) wide, made up of tubular disk flowers only; clusters top leafy branches

Leaf: oval or long, narrow leaves, 2–6" (5–15 cm) long, are succulent with pointed tips and irregularly toothed edges; variable, sometimes broad at the base, on stalks or covered with fuzzy white hairs

Bloom: summer, fall

Cycle/Origin: annual, perennial; native

Habitat: soils wet from fresh, brackish, or salty water; marshes, meadows, along streams and ponds

Range: throughout, except the far western part of Texas

Notes: A resinous, bushy plant branching in the upper portion of the single stem. Lacking petals (ray flowers) and with its pink flower parts protruding from each tiny flower (floret), the ragged-looking flower heads always appear closed. There are more than 40 species in this genus, which was named after Noël-Antoine Pluche, a French naturalist of the early 1700s. Sweetscent Camphorweed grows in more than 30 states in this country and is also found in parts of Canada. Sold in the Caribbean for medicinal purposes and as an insect repellent. Also called Salt Marsh Fleabane.

CLUSTER TYPE
Flat

FLOWER TYPE
Composite

LEAF TYPE
Simple

LEAF ATTACHMENT
Alternate

Nodding Beardtongue
Penstemon laxiflorus

Family: Snapdragon (Scrophulariaceae)

Height: 12–30" (30–76 cm)

Flower: loose spike cluster, 4–7" (10–18 cm) long, of fuzzy, drooping, pale-pink or white flowers on stalks; each tubular flower, 1" (2.5 cm) long, has 2-lobed upper and 3-lobed spreading lower petals (lips) with purplish-pink streaks

Leaf: oval or spoon-shaped basal leaves, 2–4" (5–10 cm) long, with small-toothed edges; lower leaves are stalked, upper leaves clasp the fuzzy stem

Bloom: spring, early summer

Cycle/Origin: perennial; native

Habitat: prairies, woodland clearings, fallow fields, disturbed sites, sun

Range: eastern half of Texas

Notes: Also called Loose-flowered Penstemon for the wide spacing of the flowers along the stalk. Penstemon is from the Greek words for "five" and "stamen," referring to the characteristic broad fifth flower part (stamen) that projects from the flower. This stamen has a brushy yellow tip ("beard"), thus "Beardtongue" in the common name. The purplish-pink streaks on the lower petals act as guides to point out the way to the pollen, indicating that this particular beardtongue is pollinated mainly by insects. However, Nodding Beardtongue also attracts hummingbirds.

CLUSTER TYPE
Spike

FLOWER TYPE
Tube

LEAF TYPE
Simple

LEAF ATTACHMENT
Opposite

LEAF ATTACHMENT
Clasping

LEAF ATTACHMENT
Basal

fruit

Cobaea Beardtongue

Penstemon cobaea

Family: Snapdragon (Scrophulariaceae)

Height: 12–24" (30–61 cm)

Flower: loose spike cluster, 4–8" (10–20 cm) long, of large-mouthed, pale pink-to-dark-lilac or white flowers; each balloon-like bloom, 1½–2½" (4–6 cm) long, has 5 flared lobes streaked inside with magenta

Leaf: stalkless, elliptical, or spoon-shaped leaves, 2½–6" (5–15 cm) long, with edges sharply toothed; upper leaves are smaller

Fruit: upright cup-shaped tan capsule, ½" (1 cm) long

Bloom: spring, early summer

Cycle/Origin: perennial; native

Habitat: limestone soils, prairies, fields, rocky bluffs, slopes, along streams, sun

Range: central, coastal, and northwestern Texas

Notes: A member of one of two groups of penstemons with wide flowers designed for bee pollination, providing a landing platform and a swollen tube to accommodate the chubby bodies of bumblebees. Inside, curved rigid flower parts (stamens) help hold open the mouth of the bulbous bloom. The other group has narrow tubular red flowers suited for the needle-like bills of hummingbirds. Seeded in wildflower gardens for the large, striking blooms. A tea made from the leaves was used as a laxative by early settlers.

CLUSTER TYPE	FLOWER TYPE	LEAF TYPE	LEAF ATTACHMENT	FRUIT
Spike	**Tube**	**Simple**	**Opposite**	**Pod**

Downy Paintbrush
Castilleja sessiliflora

Family: Snapdragon (Scrophulariaceae)

Height: 4–12" (10–30 cm)

Flower: many leaf-like pink bracts in a spike cluster, 4–8" (10–20 cm) long, are often mistaken for flower petals; actual flowers, 1½" (4 cm) long, are also pink but are tubular and protrude from among the bracts

Leaf: very narrow, grayish-green leaves, 1–3" (2.5–7.5 cm) long, covered with dense white hairs, densely alternate along the stem

Fruit: small pod-like green container, turning woody when mature, ½" (1 cm) long, is oblong and has pointed ends

Bloom: spring, summer

Cycle/Origin: perennial; native

Habitat: prairies, along roads, rocky hillsides, sun

Range: western Texas

Notes: The leaves, stems, and flowers of this very leafy wildflower are covered with dense, short, white hairs, thus "Downy" in the common name. Genus is named for the 16th century Spanish botanist Domingo Castillejo. Often cultivated and used in borders, but needs to be planted near other plants (often asters or junipers) to absorb nutrients from their roots (semiparasitic). Found in the Southwest and ranges north through the prairie states and into Canada.

CLUSTER TYPE	FLOWER TYPE	LEAF TYPE	LEAF ATTACHMENT	FRUIT
Spike	**Tube**	**Simple**	**Alternate**	**Pod**

149

Winged Lythrum
Lythrum alatum

Family: Loosestrife (Lythraceae)

Height: 2–3½' (61–107 cm)

Flower: long spike cluster, 4–10" (10–25 cm) long, of purplish-rose flowers; each tubular flower, ½" (1 cm) wide, has 4–6 purple-veined petals around a purple-and-green center; flowers grow in pairs or singly on a short stalk from upper leaf attachments (axis)

Leaf: narrow or broadly lance-shaped leaves, 1–2½" (2.5–6 cm) long; upper leaves are usually alternate, lower are mostly opposite; stalkless leaves nearly clasp the 4-angled, slightly winged stem

Bloom: summer, fall

Cycle/Origin: perennial; native

Habitat: rich soils, wet areas; along streams, ponds, and swamps; ditches, prairies

Range: eastern, central, and southern Texas

Notes: A beautiful wildflower often growing in large colonies, Spreads by sending out new shoots from the stem. "Winged" refers to the shallow wings on each of the four ribs of the stem. One of the few species that has both opposite and alternate leaves on the same plant. Many types of long-tongued insects visit the flowers, including bee flies, butterflies, and many bee species. This desirable native plant should not be confused with Purple Loosestrife (*L. salicaria;* not shown), an aggressive Eurasian weed that invades wetlands.

CLUSTER TYPE	FLOWER TYPE	LEAF TYPE	LEAF ATTACHMENT	LEAF ATTACHMENT
Spike	**Tube**	**Simple**	**Alternate**	**Opposite**

151

Canada Germander
Teucrium canadense

Family: Mint (Lamiaceae)

Height: 12–36" (30–91 cm)

Flower: pale-pink spike cluster, 5–12" (13–30 cm) long, blooms from bottom up with dense rings of flowers; each bloom, ¾" (2 cm) long, has 5 spotted petals fused at base and flaring into short upper and broad 3-lobed lower petals (lips); curved flower parts (stamens) protrude from a notch in upper lip

Leaf: broad lance-shaped crinkled leaves, 2–6" (5–15 cm) long, are stalked, coarsely toothed, and have dense hairs below; square stout stem is rough and fuzzy

Bloom: spring, summer, fall

Cycle/Origin: perennial; native

Habitat: rich moist soils, prairies, meadows, marshes

Range: throughout

Notes: Spreading by underground stems (rhizomes), this flashy perennial can form large colonies and become quite weedy. Found throughout the United States and Canada wherever fertile soil is consistently wet, as it cannot tolerate much drought. Darker pink spots on the broadest lobe of the flower's lower lip act like runway lights on a landing platform, guiding insects to the pollen. Can be confused with other mints, but the complex form of the lower lip and extremely short upper lip identify this species. Sometimes called Wood Sage or American Germander.

CLUSTER TYPE
Spike

FLOWER TYPE
Irregular

LEAF TYPE
Simple

LEAF ATTACHMENT
Opposite

153

Copper Globemallow
Sphaeralcea angustifolia

Family: Mallow (Malvaceae)

Height: 3–6' (.9–1.8 m)

Flower: wand-like spike cluster, 6–12" (15–30 cm) long, of many coppery pink, bowl-shaped flowers; each blossom, 1½" (4 cm) wide, has 5 triangular petals around a yellow-and-green center; flower color can also be coral pink, orange, apricot, or purple

Leaf: wrinkled, hairy, narrow leaves; 1½–4" (4–10 cm) long, are grayish green, folded lengthwise, long-stalked, and have coarse-toothed wavy margins

Bloom: spring, summer, fall

Cycle/Origin: perennial; native

Habitat: limestone soils, prairies, rocky slopes, pastures, along fences

Range: western half of Texas

Notes: A stout, hairy perennial with numerous unbranched stems that bear flowers in clusters at the leaf junctions along the upper stalks. As in all mallows, the flowers have many flower parts (stamens) fused to form a slim column. The stamens are yellow in this species. Star-shaped white hairs cover the foliage, giving it a soft, grayish-green appearance. Historically, the stems were chewed as a gum. Deer graze upon the foliage. Sometimes called Narrowleaf Globemallow for the slim leaves. Found throughout the Southwest, from southern California to Kansas and south into Mexico.

CLUSTER TYPE	FLOWER TYPE	LEAF TYPE	LEAF ATTACHMENT
Spike	**Regular**	**Simple**	**Alternate**

Drummond Onion
Allium drummondii

Family: Lily (Liliaceae)

Height: 4–12" (10–30 cm)

Flower: loose round clusters, 8–20" (20–50 cm) wide, of 10–25 light pink-to-dark-rose flowers; each star-shaped flower, ¾" (2 cm) wide, has 6 slightly cupped and pointed petals; clusters tip the leafless, hollow flower stalks

Leaf: 3–4 grass-like leaves, 4–12" (10–30 cm) long, grow from the base and have a shallow V-shaped channel running lengthwise

Fruit: 3–celled capsule held in nodding brown seed head

Bloom: spring, summer

Cycle/Origin: perennial; native

Habitat: limestone soils, prairies, woodland openings, canyons, hillsides, along roads

Range: throughout

Notes: Sometimes called Prairie Onion for where it grows, this is the most widespread onion in Texas. The bulbs contain inulin, a sugar that cannot be digested by humans unless the bulbs are first cooked for a long time. Once added to meat dishes by the Plains Indians. Sandhill Cranes feed on the new leaves in spring. The small bulbs in a mesh-like covering can be divided to grow new plants, which also can be grown from seed. Drought-tolerant once established. Sometimes grown for its delicate pink flowers.

CLUSTER TYPE **Round** FLOWER TYPE **Regular** LEAF TYPE **Simple** LEAF ATTACHMENT **Basal** FRUIT **Pod**

Scarlet Pea
Indigofera miniata

Family: Pea or Bean (Fabaceae)

Height: 12–36" (30–91 cm)

Flower: upright, salmon pink-to-scarlet-red spike cluster, 8–25" (20–64 cm) long, of 8–25 small flowers, ¾" (2 cm) long, blooming from the bottom of the spike upward and forming a ring; flower spikes emerge above the leaves

Leaf: fuzzy, pale-green or dark-green leaves, 3" (7.5 cm) long, are divided into 5–9 teardrop-shaped leaflets, 1" (2.5 cm) long; white-haired green stems

Fruit: straight or angled slender green pod, 1½" (4 cm) long, turns brown when mature

Bloom: spring, summer, fall

Cycle/Origin: perennial; native

Habitat: sandy well-drained soils, prairies, lawns, fields, open woods, dunes

Range: eastern two-thirds of Texas

Notes: An abundant legume with trailing, spreading stems from a woody base. Ground-hugging mats of this attractive pea range from Texas north to Kansas and east to Florida. Although the flowers are usually some shade of pink, they can be red, thus "Scarlet" in the common name. Sometimes called Texas Indigo. Grown in butterfly gardens, as it is a host plant for caterpillars of Gray Hairstreak butterflies and several species of tiny blue butterflies.

CLUSTER TYPE	FLOWER TYPE	LEAF TYPE	LEAF ATTACHMENT	FRUIT
Spike	**Irregular**	**Compound**	**Alternate**	**Pod**

Smallflower Milkvetch
Astragalus nuttallianus

Family: Pea or Bean (Fabaceae)

Height: 6–12" (15–30 cm)

Flower: small, pea-like purple flower, ¼–½" (.6–1 cm) long, has an upright, purple-to-blue upper petal (standard) with a large purple-veined white spot; 1–7 blooms grouped at end of the stems

Leaf: feather-like leaves, 3" (7.5 cm) long, are divided into 7–15 white-haired, narrowly oval leaflets; upright or trailing, reddish-green stems

Fruit: smooth or hairy, curved slender pod, 1" (2.5 cm) long, is green and turns red when mature; pods are horizontal from the stem tips

Bloom: early spring, early summer

Cycle/Origin: annual; native

Habitat: sandy soils of deserts, prairies, plateaus, woodlands

Range: throughout

Notes: One of the most widespread milkvetches in Texas, there are more than 30 similar milkvetch species found in the state. Variable, it can grow in mats of sprawling stems sometimes less than 1 inch (2.5 cm) tall or have upright stems reaching a height of 12 inches (30 cm). Flower color also varies from white to light or neon blue, or from pink to purple. Ranges from California east to Oklahoma and south to Mexico. Toxic to livestock, causing weight loss, inability to control the hind legs or total paralysis.

FLOWER TYPE	LEAF TYPE	LEAF ATTACHMENT	FRUIT
Irregular	**Compound**	**Alternate**	**Pod**

Bristly Nama

Nama hispidum

Family: Waterleaf (Hydrophyllaceae)

Height: 3–12" (7.5–30 cm)

Flower: upright tube flower, ½" (1 cm) wide, appears as a regular flower from above, but is actually tubular with 5 rounded spreading lobes; blooms are purple to reddish pink to pink-and-white, each with a pale-yellow throat

Leaf: long and narrow to spoon-shaped leaves, ½–2" (1–5 cm) long, are grayish green, sticky, hairy, with blunt tips; edges partially rolled under; ends of sprawling, branching stems grow upright

Bloom: spring, summer

Cycle/Origin: annual; native

Habitat: sandy soils, roadsides

Range: throughout, except the far eastern portion of Texas

Notes: Bristly Nama is extremely common and abundant, forming mats that can carpet large areas after heavy rains. In drought years, only a few plants producing a handful of flowers grow wherever extra moisture is still available. This species is sometimes called Sandbells due to its preference for sandy soils and for the tubular flowers with widely spreading lobes, resembling upright bells. When cultivated and with added water, it makes a good, low-growing ground cover that blooms profusely throughout the summer.

FLOWER TYPE	LEAF TYPE	LEAF ATTACHMENT
Tube	**Simple**	**Alternate**

Drummond Skullcap

Scutellaria drummondii

Family: Mint (Lamiaceae)

Height: 8–12" (20–30 cm)

Flower: pairs of pale-purple or dark-bluish-purple flowers; each tube-shaped flower, ½" (1 cm) long, has a fuzzy bulbous upper petal (lip) forming a "hood" over the broader lower lip with 2 purple-dotted white spots and is held by 2 round maroon sepals

Leaf: soft oval leaves, ½" (1 cm) long, with smooth edges, on short stalks; square stem is slightly hairy

Bloom: spring, summer

Cycle/Origin: annual, perennial; native

Habitat: prairies, mesas, rocky hillsides, along railroads

Range: throughout Texas, except the far eastern portion of the state

Notes: A short, fuzzy plant branching at the base into many stems. Often found in weedy areas. Sometimes the flowers never open, self-pollinating and setting seed while closed. The leaves and flowers (when they do open) lack fragrance, unlike most other types of mints. Scutellaria is from the Latin word for "dish" or "skullcap" and describes the bulbous upper lip, which has a cap shape that resembles a monk's headgear. The species name is for Thomas Drummond, one of the first plant collectors to explore Texas. Interestingly, recent studies have isolated chemicals from this wildflower that have antifungal and insect repellent properties.

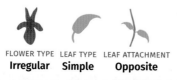

FLOWER TYPE **Irregular**   LEAF TYPE **Simple**   LEAF ATTACHMENT **Opposite**

165

Field Pansy
Viola bicolor

Family: Violet (Violaceae)

Height: 2–8" (5–20 cm)

Flower: variable color (can be purple, blue, pink, cream, or white), ½–¾" (1–2 cm) wide, with a yellow-and-white throat, 5 unequal-size petals (lower 3 are purple-streaked); single flowers on flower stalks

Leaf: round or oval basal leaves, ½" (1 cm) wide, have shallowly notched edges and are stalked; larger, spoon-shaped stem leaves are deeply lobed; leaf-like appendages (stipules) ring stem at each leaf axis

Bloom: very early to late spring

Cycle/Origin: annual; native

Habitat: dry to moist sandy soils, pastures, lawns, along railroads and roads, fencerows, disturbed sites

Range: northeastern corner of Texas

Notes: Also called Johnny-jump-up for its rapid growth and sudden appearance in spring. In years with good winter rains, can be found in large colonies along roads mixed with Tiny Bluet (pg. 77) and Spring Beauty (pg. 85). There are 18 species of wild violet in Texas, and hybrids are common, making identification difficult. More heat resistant than the common garden pansy, Field Pansy is readily available for purchase, but beware–plants sold as Johnny-jump-up in garden centers are a European species (*V. tricolor*). Plants in the Violet family are host plants for fritillary butterfly caterpillars.

FLOWER TYPE
Irregular

LEAF TYPE
Simple

LEAF ATTACHMENT
Alternate

LEAF ATTACHMENT
Basal

fruit

Snapdragonvine
Maurandella antirrhiniflora

Family: Snapdragon (Scrophulariaceae)

Height: 3–10' (.9–3 m); vine

Flower: snapdragon-like purple flower, ½–¾" (1–2 cm) long, has 2 upper upright lobes, 3 lower lobes, a triangular swollen white throat with a hairy bump lined with purple, and a spotted tube; 5 pointed green sepals

Leaf: broad arrowhead-shaped leaves, ½–2" (1–5 cm) long, are dark to bright green, on a twining stem

Fruit: round green pod, ⅓" (.8 cm) wide, turning reddish brown, has a thread-like stem in middle; pod cupped by 5 pointed, persistent sepals

Bloom: spring, summer, fall

Cycle/Origin: perennial; native

Habitat: deserts, woodlands, flats, slopes

Range: southwestern third of Texas

Notes: This delicate-looking vine is often cultivated in Texas for its beautiful, small flowers, which can also be blue or reddish pink. Snapdragonvine has ivy-like leaves and grows well when planted in a pot with a trellis. A food plant for Common Buckeye butterfly caterpillars, thus it is also planted in butterfly gardens. Usually deciduous, dying off in winter and growing from the root in spring. However, it is semi-evergreen in some protected habitats.

FLOWER TYPE
Tube

LEAF TYPE
Simple

LEAF ATTACHMENT
Alternate

FRUIT
Pod

169

Bluebowls

Giliastrum rigidulum

Family: Phlox (Polemoniaceae)

Height: 3–10" (7.5–25 cm)

Flower: bowl-shaped, bluish-purple flower (can be pale or dark in color), ¾" (2 cm) wide, has 5 wide petals with pointed or rounded tips; yellow center outlined with white and protruding yellow flower parts; 1 to several blossoms from leaf junctions of branching slim stem

Leaf: dense needle-like leaves, ½–1" (1–2.5 cm) long, have smooth margins or are deeply divided into 3–7 short thin lobes

Bloom: spring, summer, fall

Cycle/Origin: annual, perennial; native

Habitat: dry, rocky soils with calcium carbonate (caliche); prairies, hillsides, thickets

Range: central, southern, and northwestern Texas

Notes: The petals of this distinctive wildflower can be pointed or rounded, but the flowers are always eye-catching with their bluish-violet petals and bright-yellow-and-white centers, which serve to guide insects to the pollen. Slim, rigid, green stems are upright or sprawling and widely branching. Plant seeds in wildflower gardens for abundant spring flowers that continue to bloom intermittently until autumn. Native to Texas, New Mexico, and northern Mexico.

FLOWER TYPE
Regular

LEAF TYPE
Simple

LEAF TYPE
Simple Lobed

LEAF ATTACHMENT
Alternate

LEAF ATTACHMENT
Basal

171

Clasping Venus's Looking Glass
Triodanis perfoliata

Family: Bellflower (Campanulaceae)

Height: 4–24" (10–61 cm)

Flower: star-shaped, bluish purple-to-lavender flower (can be bright blue), ¾" (2 cm) wide, made up of 5 oblong pointed petals (sometimes streaked with white) around a paler center

Leaf: heart-shaped leaves, up to 1" (2.5 cm) long, have rounded tips and blunt-toothed margins; upper leaves are much smaller than lower; 5–angled, deeply grooved stem has white hairs

Bloom: spring, summer

Cycle/Origin: annual; native

Habitat: disturbed areas, pastures, prairies, woodland edges

Range: throughout

Notes: Also called Roundleaf Triodanis or Clasping Bellflower, with both names referring to the rounded leaves that clasp the stem. "Looking Glass" in the common name refers to the reflectiveness of the shiny black seeds. Although in the Bellflower family, the petals are horizontal or slightly upright, not fused together into a bell shape and hanging downward, as is typical of those in the family. Like others in the Triodanis genus, the upper flowers open for pollination, while the lower flowers stay closed and are self-pollinating. Attracts small butterflies, bees, and flies.

FLOWER TYPE **Regular**   LEAF TYPE **Simple**   LEAF ATTACHMENT **Alternate**   LEAF ATTACHMENT **Clasping**

fruit

Silverleaf Nightshade
Solanum elaeagnifolium

Family: Nightshade (Solanaceae)

Height: 1–4' (30–122 cm)

Flower: loose groups of star-shaped purple (sometimes white) flowers; each flower, ¾–1½" (2–4 cm) wide, has 5 long, triangular fused petals that are wrinkled and thin, with wavy edges surrounding the bright-yellow protruding flower parts (stamens)

Leaf: narrowly lance-shaped leaves, 2–6" (5–15 cm) long, greenish gray with wavy margins and orange spines on veins below; long, straight thorns on stems

Fruit: round berry-like fruit, ⅓–⅔" (.8–1.6 cm) wide, is smooth and hard; mottled green, turning orangish yellow when ripe; dangles from thorny stalk

Bloom: spring, summer, fall

Cycle/Origin: perennial; native

Habitat: very dry soils, deserts, prairies, disturbed areas

Range: throughout

Notes: The silvery gray cast to the leaves and stems is from a covering of dense, star-shaped hairs. An invasive weed toxic to livestock. Spreads by deep underground stems (rhizomes) and forms colonies that are hard to eradicate. The plant, containing a digestive enzyme, historically was combined with animal brain tissue and used to tan hides. American Indians used the crushed fruit to curdle milk when making cheese.

FLOWER TYPE   LEAF TYPE   LEAF ATTACHMENT   FRUIT
Regular   **Simple**   **Alternate**   **Berry**

Polkadots
Dyschoriste linearis

Family: Acanthus (Acanthaceae)

Height: 6–12" (15–30 cm)

Flower: upright bell-shaped flowers, 1" (2.5 cm) wide, purple to lavender, each with 5 petals fused at base into a short tube and flaring at mouth into 2 upper and 3 lower lobes; purple spots or streaks in throat; single flowers atop short stalks tucked among leaves along the stem

Leaf: rigid, narrowly oblong leaves, ¾–2¾" (2–7 cm) long, have margins fringed with hairs and are stalkless; coarsely haired, unbranched square stems

Bloom: spring, summer, early fall

Cycle/Origin: perennial; native

Habitat: dry, sandy soils; rocky grassy hillsides, prairies

Range: throughout, except the far eastern and northwestern portions of Texas

Notes: Named for the purple dots or streaks in the white throat of the flower. Forming wide colonies from spreading underground stems (rhizomes), this little plant grows in dense mounds of hairy, narrow leaves and petunia-like purple flowers. Sometimes called Narrowleaf Snakeherb. Frequently cultivated, as it tolerates poor soil in full sun and dry conditions. The fruit is a small, two-celled capsule that opens explosively when ripe. The seeds are attached to a small hooked stalk that ejects them from the capsule.

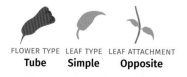

FLOWER TYPE
Tube

LEAF TYPE
Simple

LEAF ATTACHMENT
Opposite

Leavenworth Eryngo
Eryngium leavenworthii

Family: Carrot (Apiaceae)

Height: 20–36" (50–91 cm)

Flower: thick and fuzzy spike cluster, 1" (2.5 cm) long, of densely packed, tiny purple flowers with protruding purple flower parts (stamens); flowers among miniature purple bracts; whorls of larger spiny purple bracts at top and bottom of cluster; blooms top the branches of upper stem

Leaf: segmented spiny leaves, 1–2½" (2.5–6 cm) long, are deeply divided into spine-tipped irregular lobes and clasp the stout stem; basal rosette of spoon-shaped, smooth-edged leaves wilt by flowering time

Bloom: summer, fall

Cycle/Origin: annual; native

Habitat: dry sandy, clay, or limestone soils; prairies, fields

Range: central Texas

Notes: Appears similar to garden lettuce when it first sprouts, but then shoots up a stout stalk that branches only at the tip, bearing flower clusters. The green clusters and stem turn all red, then deep purple with age. It is sometimes confused with a thistle due to its spininess and color. This unique, spectacular plant can cover acres of grasslands with purple in late summer and autumn. The nectar of the minute flowers attracts butterflies, and finches eat the resulting seeds. Deer and livestock avoid the spiny foliage.

STER TYPE	FLOWER TYPE	LEAF TYPE	LEAF TYPE	LEAF ATTACHMENT	LEAF ATTACHMENT
Spike	**Regular**	**Simple**	**Simple Lobed**	**Alternate**	**Basal**

fruit

Filaree
Erodium cicutarium

Family: Geranium (Geraniaceae)

Height: 4–20" (10–50 cm)

Flower: loose, flat cluster, 1" (2.5 cm) wide, of 2–12 violet-to-pink flowers; each small flower is ¼" (.6 cm) wide and has 5 oval petals backed by 5 pointed, hairy sepals; each sepal is green with white lines

Leaf: lance- or kidney-shaped, reddish- or dark-green basal leaves, 2–10" (5–25 cm) long, in a prostrate rosette, fern-like, fuzzy, divided into lobed leaflets

Fruit: upright green capsule, ¾–2" (2–5 cm) long, turning brown, is long, pointed, and shaped like the beak of a heron or stork; twists into a spiral when dry

Bloom: early spring, summer

Cycle/Origin: annual, biennial; nonnative, from southern Europe

Habitat: disturbed soils, roadsides

Range: western two-thirds of Texas

Notes: A miniature geranium, Filaree is often the first weed to overtake any disturbed soils, such as overgrazed rangelands, and can reduce crop production. Also named Redstem Stork's Bill for the shape of the seedpod. The pod curls into a corkscrew shape when dry, looking like a tail on the seed; it untwists when moistened by rain, which drives the single seed into the ground. Seeds are eaten by harvester ants and birds. Desert Tortoises, Bighorn Sheep, deer, and livestock eat the foliage.

USTER TYPE	FLOWER TYPE	LEAF TYPE	LEAF ATTACHMENT	LEAF ATTACHMENT	FRUIT
Flat	**Regular**	**Compound**	**Opposite**	**Basal**	**Pod**

Trailing Four O'clock
Allionia incarnata

Family: Four O'clock (Nyctaginaceae)

Height: 1–5' (30–152 cm); vine

Flower: appears to be a regular flower, 1" (2.5 cm) wide, composed of 9 flat, 2–lobed, pinkish-purple petals surrounding a magenta-and-yellow center, but is actually made up of 3 irregular flowers on a short stalk growing from a leaf attachment

Leaf: oval leaves, ¾–3" (2–7.5 cm) long, are dull green above, gray below, and have blunt bases, usually pointed tips and smooth or wavy edges; pairs of leaves are of unequal size; sticky, hairy stem

Bloom: any season after rainfall, except when very cold

Cycle/Origin: annual, perennial; native

Habitat: dry, sandy, or gravelly limestone soils, deserts, prairies, along roads and washes, slopes

Range: western half of Texas

Notes: This ground-hugging vine has flowers that each appear to be one regular, round, and flat blossom, but which are actually three irregular flowers blooming at the same time. Blooms after rain in all but the coldest weather. Occurs wherever there is sandy soil, often in disturbed areas. The sticky, hairy leaves are usually dotted with sand. American Indians used this plant as a poultice to treat swelling and fever, and brewed it into a tea to treat diarrhea or kidney disease. Trailing Four-O'clock occurs throughout the Southwest.

FLOWER TYPE **Irregular** LEAF TYPE **Simple** LEAF ATTACHMENT **Opposite**

183

Meadow Aster
Symphyotrichum pratense

Family: Aster (Asteraceae)

Height: 20–32" (50–80 cm)

Flower: purple-and-yellow flower head, 1–1½" (2.5–4 cm) wide, has 15–25 purple petals (ray flowers) with a yellow center (disk flowers) that becomes reddish brown after pollination; a few single blossoms top the leafy, sticky-haired flower stalk

Leaf: many stalkless lance-shaped leaves, ½–1" (1–2.5 cm) long; lower and upper leaves are the same size

Bloom: fall

Cycle/Origin: perennial; native

Habitat: sandy soils, prairies, meadows, edges of thickets and woodlands, open areas along creeks, sun

Range: central, eastern, and coastal Texas

Notes: A showy, autumn-blooming plant, Meadow Aster features a single upright stiff stem with a few branches near the top and a few large, rich purple-to-violet blooms. Sometimes called Barrens Silky Aster for the open areas where it grows and the long soft hairs on the leaves and stems. A great nectar plant because of its long blooming time in the fall. Heavily visited by migrating Monarch butterflies. Grows wild throughout much of the southern United States from Texas east to North Carolina and Florida, but is rare in Kentucky and Georgia.

FLOWER TYPE **Composite** LEAF TYPE **Simple** LEAF ATTACHMENT **Alternate**

Tansyleaf Tansyaster
Machaeranthera tanacetifolia

Family: Aster (Asteraceae)

Height: 4–16" (10–40 cm)

Flower: bluish-violet flower head, 1–2" (2.5–5 cm) wide, is daisy-like and has 12–40 narrow petals (ray flowers) surrounding a yellow center (disk flowers)

Leaf: dense feathery leaves, ⅓–4½" (.8–11 cm) long, are grayish green, sticky, hairy, and highly divided into opposite pairs of lobes; each lobe is tipped with bristly hairs; reddish-green stems are also hairy

Bloom: spring, summer, fall

Cycle/Origin: annual; native

Habitat: disturbed areas, deserts, prairies, along streams or roads

Range: northwestern and far western Texas

Notes: There are seven species of tansyaster in the genus Machaeranthera in Texas, recognizable by the spiny bristle at the tip of each leaf lobe. The Greek words machaer and anthera in the genus name refer to the sword shape of the tips of the flower parts (anthers). This tansyaster can be identified by its fern-like or feathery leaves. It is often cultivated from seed for the many showy flowers and sold under the name Tahoka Daisy.

FLOWER TYPE
Composite

LEAF TYPE
Simple Lobed

LEAF ATTACHMENT
Alternate

Alfalfa
Medicago sativa

Family: Pea or Bean (Fabaceae)

Height: 12–36" (30–91 cm)

Flower: tight spike cluster, 1–2" (2.5–5 cm) long, of deep purple-to-dark-blue flowers (color can range to light blue); each small flower, ¼–⅓" (.6–.8 cm) long, has a 1 large upper petal and 3 smaller lower petals

Leaf: 3–parted and clover-like, 1–2" (2.5–5 cm) long, with sharp-toothed margins near tips

Fruit: downy green seedpod that twists into coils, turning nearly black with age

Bloom: spring, summer, fall

Cycle/Origin: perennial; nonnative

Habitat: agricultural areas, abandoned fields, along roads

Range: throughout

Notes: This deep-rooted plant is usually found in irrigated fields or along roads where it has escaped cultivation. Often planted by farmers in Texas as a food crop for livestock and to improve soil fertility. Alfalfa hay is a favorite of horses and is often fed to them—sometimes to their detriment, as it contains a high percentage of protein that can lead to laminitis (a disease affecting hooves). Prime host plant for Orange Sulphur butterfly caterpillars. Countless adult Orange Sulphurs hovering above a field of blooming alfalfa look like a swarm of dancing orange flowers.

CLUSTER TYPE	FLOWER TYPE	LEAF TYPE	LEAF ATTACHMENT	FRUIT
Spike	**Irregular**	**Compound**	**Alternate**	**Pod**

Wild Bergamot
Monarda fistulosa

Family: Mint (Lamiaceae)

Height: 2–4' (61–122 cm)

Flower: many pale-lavender flowers in a round cluster, 1–2" (2.5–5 cm) wide; each flower, 1" (2.5 cm) long, has 2 petals (lips) with the upper lip tipped with a tuft of hairs; clusters sit atop the stems and branches

Leaf: lance-shaped leaves, 1–3" (2.5–7.5 cm) long, that taper to pointed tips and have coarse-toothed margins; each leaf is on a short leafstalk, oppositely attached to a square, red stem

Bloom: spring, summer

Cycle/Origin: perennial; native

Habitat: moist, sandy, or rocky soils in old fields, wooded slopes, forest edges, mountain canyons, roadsides

Range: eastern and far western Texas

Notes: Also called Horsemint or Bee Balm, this is a tall plant of open areas and roadsides. Look for its square stems and oppositely attached leaves to help identify. Emits a strong scent when any part of the plant is rubbed or crushed. The fragrance of the flower heads attracts many insects, including bees, butterflies, and beetles. "Bergamot" refers to a small citrus tree that produces a scent similar to that of this plant. Once used in folk medicine to make a mint tea to treat many respiratory and digestive ailments. Its oil is an essential flavoring in Earl Grey tea.

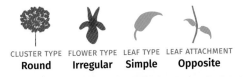

CLUSTER TYPE	FLOWER TYPE	LEAF TYPE	LEAF ATTACHMENT
Round	**Irregular**	**Simple**	**Opposite**

Spurred Butterfly Pea
Centrosema virginianum

Family: Pea or Bean (Fabaceae)

Height: 2–5' (61–152 cm); vine

Flower: large, odd-shaped, pink-to-lavender flower, 1½" (4 cm) wide, made of 5 dissimilar petals with a white streak in center of the 2 broadest joined petals; only 1 of 4 flowers blooms at a time; flowers loosely arranged on a short flower stalk

Leaf: compound leaves with its 3 pointed oval leaflets, each 1–3" (2.5–7.5 cm) long, resemble a turkey's foot; leaves alternately attached to twining stem

Fruit: thin, flat, stalkless green pod, 3–5" (7.5–13 cm) long; after releasing seeds, the dry brown pod with its tightly curled sides remains on vine

Bloom: spring, summer, fall

Cycle/Origin: perennial; native

Habitat: dry, sandy soils; open woods, thicket edges, fields, along roads

Range: eastern half of Texas

Notes: This climbing or trailing vine is relatively low growing and often cultivated for its pretty flowers, which are conspicuous. The loose clusters of blooms hang upside down from the leaf attachments (axis). Like most plants in the Pea or Bean family, Spurred Butterfly Pea has nodules of bacteria on its roots that fix the nitrogen into the soil, thus improving soil fertility for plants.

FLOWER TYPE
Irregular

LEAF TYPE
Compound

LEAF ATTACHMENT
Alternate

FRUIT
Pod

fruit

Bluebill
Clematis pitcheri

Family: Buttercup (Ranunculaceae)

Height: 5–10' (1.5–3 m); vine

Flower: bell-shaped purple flowers, 1½" (4 cm) long; each nodding bloom has 4 thick, pointed, petal-like sepals fused at the base, flaring widely at the mouth, and curving backward; fuzzy, yellow center; 1 to several flowers on long stalks from leaf junctions

Leaf: compound leaves on long stalks and divided into 3–5 lobed broad leaflets on stalks; each leaflet, 3–4" (7.5–10 cm) long; end (terminal) leaflet modified into a twining tendril; some leaves are undivided

Fruit: flattened, beaked containers in a spider-like whorl; each container has 1 seed; light green or burgundy, drying and turning brownish black with age

Bloom: late winter, spring

Cycle/Origin: perennial; native

Habitat: sandy soils, along creeks or streams, crevices of canyons, climbing in shrubs or over boulders

Range: throughout, except the northeastern part of Texas

Notes: The thick, wrinkled sepals of the flowers appear leathery, thus another common name, Leatherflower. The leaflets of the compound leaves are so large that they are often mistaken for the leaves. Tendrils at the ends of terminal leaflets enable this somewhat woody vine to cling to other plants and fences. Pollinated by bumblebees.

FLOWER TYPE
Bell

LEAF TYPE
Simple

LEAF TYPE
Compound

LEAF ATTACHMENT
Opposite

FRUIT
Pod

195

Dakota Mock Vervain
Glandularia bipinnatifida

Family: Verbena (Verbenaceae)

Height: 6–18" (15–45 cm)

Flower: violet-to-pink flat cluster, 1½" (4 cm) wide, of many small flowers, ½" (1 cm) wide; each flower looks like a gingerbread man with its 5 notched petals that are each a slightly differently shape

Leaf: dark-green or bluish-green leaves, ¾–2½" (2–6 cm) long, are hairy and deeply cut into lobes, with edges curled under; oppositely attached to the hairy stem

Bloom: early spring, summer

Cycle/Origin: annual, perennial; native

Habitat: prairies, woodlands, under pine trees, along roads and washes

Range: throughout Texas, except the far eastern part of the state

Notes: The abundant nectar of these beautiful, long-blooming flowers attracts butterflies, thus this plant is frequently cultivated in butterfly or rock gardens. Dakota Mock Vervain is hardy and drought-tolerant. Its sprawling stems result in mats covering large barren areas, making the plant a good choice for ground cover.

CLUSTER TYPE
Flat

FLOWER TYPE
Irregular

LEAF TYPE
Simple Lobed

LEAF ATTACHMENT
Opposite

197

fruit

Purple Passionflower
Passiflora incarnata

Family: Passionflower (Passifloraceae)

Height: 7–26' (2.1–7.9 m); vine

Flower: intricate, solitary, lavender flowers (can be pink and white), 1½–2½" (4–6 cm) wide, each with 10 similar elliptical petals below a fringed crown of wavy white or lavender filaments around a band of purple or pink that surrounds a green or white center

Leaf: broad, dark-green leaves, 2½–6" (6–15 cm) long, with 3 deep lobes and fine-toothed edges; sticky tendrils at leaf attachments

Fruit: green pod, the shape and size of a chicken's egg, 2–3" (5–7.5 cm) long, turns yellow when ripe

Bloom: spring, summer, early fall

Cycle/Origin: perennial; native

Habitat: disturbed areas, old pastures, edges of streams

Range: eastern and central Texas and along the coast

Notes: This exotic-looking wildflower has many common names including Maypop, for the popping sounds the pod makes when squashed. American Indians and early settlers ate the fruit or used it in drinks, ate young leaves as greens, and used the roots in medicines. The fruit (called passion fruit) is still used in beverages. Planting it in a garden almost guarantees the arrival of the bright-orange Gulf Fritillary butterfly, which lays its eggs on the leaves. The resulting caterpillars require passionflower leaves as food to grow.

FLOWER TYPE
Regular

LEAF TYPE
Simple Lobed

LEAF ATTACHMENT
Alternate

FRUIT
Pod

Fringed Twinevine
Funastrum cynanchoides

Family: Milkweed (Asclepiadaceae)

Height: 8–40' (2.4–12.2 m); vine

Flower: round cluster, 1½–4" (4–10 cm) wide, pinkish purple or white, of 15–25 star-shaped flowers; each flower, ½" (1 cm) wide, has 5 pointed, fuzzy-edged, pinkish purple-and-white petals and 5 sepals around a white protruding center made up of 5 inflated sacs

Leaf: variable-shaped leaves, ½–2½" (1–6 cm) long, with pointed or rounded tips and blunt or lobed bases

Fruit: narrow, purplish-green pod, turning brown, 1½–3½" (4–9 cm) long, is pointed at both ends, bulges in the middle and contains reddish-brown seeds

Bloom: spring, summer, early fall

Cycle/Origin: perennial; native

Habitat: disturbed sites, thickets, deserts, prairies, on rocky cliffs, ravines

Range: western two-thirds of Texas

Notes: When broken or cut, the stems of this milkweed exude a white sap that smells foul and can irritate skin on contact. Grows from a large main root, which is hard to dig out; it will grow again from any small root piece left in the soil. Thus, although native, it can be an invasive weed in gardens and yards. The small seeds are attached to downy tufts that act as parachutes, which carry the seeds away on the wind, so it spreads readily from one area to another.

CLUSTER TYPE	FLOWER TYPE	LEAF TYPE	LEAF ATTACHMENT	FRUIT
Round	**Regular**	**Simple**	**Opposite**	**Pod**

Prairie Nymph
Herbertia lahue

Family: Iris (Iridaceae)

Height: 5–12" (13–30 cm)

Flower: pale purple-to-dark-purple flowers, 2" (5 cm) wide; each has 3 large propeller-like petals with dark-purple spots on their white bases, around 3 much smaller pointed petals with dark-violet bases; 1–3 flowers from a green bract atop slim flower stalk

Leaf: flexible grass-like basal leaves, up to 12" (30 cm) long, are folded lengthwise and have pointed tips; usually 3 leaves per plant

Fruit: paddle-shaped green capsule, turning brown, ¾" (2 cm) long, opens at the top when mature

Bloom: spring, early summer

Cycle/Origin: perennial; native

Habitat: pastures, woodland openings, oak savannahs

Range: south central, far southern, southeastern, and coastal Texas

Notes: This short iris forms a miniature clump of narrow leaves topped with stunning, colorful flowers that bloom throughout the spring. The outer petals resemble propellers on an old-fashioned prop plane, thus another common name, Propeller Plant. Can form single-species colonies covering more than 50 acres (20 ha) when growing in sandy or clay soils, especially those of coastal prairies. Prairie Nymph is easily cultivated from seeds or bulbs.

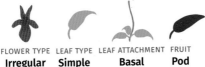

FLOWER TYPE	LEAF TYPE	LEAF ATTACHMENT	FRUIT
Irregular	**Simple**	**Basal**	**Pod**

Purple Deadnettle
Lamium purpureum

Family: Mint (Lamiaceae)

Height: 2–8" (5–20 cm)

Flower: dense whorls, 2" (5 cm) wide, made up of 3 pale pinkish-purple flowers mostly hidden below purplish-green bracts, are near top of stem; each small blossom, ⅝" (1.5 cm) long, has 1 fuzzy, hood-like upper lobe and 2 lower lobes with dark rose spots

Leaf: triangular, wrinkled, grayish-green leaves, 1–2" (2.5–5 cm) long, with round-toothed edges; new upper leaves are purple-tinged and stalkless, lower leaves have stalks; square, hollow, reddish-green stem

Bloom: spring, summer

Cycle/Origin: annual; nonnative

Habitat: disturbed soils, lawns, old fields, roadsides

Range: eastern Texas

Notes: This non-fragrant, low-growing member of the Mint family was introduced from Europe and Asia and has escaped cultivation. Now found in most of the United States and Canada. Sometimes covering acres with purple and pink color, it often grows alongside of and is easily mistaken for Henbit Deadnettle (pg. 131). Distinguish between the two by the flowers—Purple Deadnettle's are nearly hidden below the bracts, while those of Henbit Deadnettle conspicuously protrude above the bracts. Young plants have edible tops and leaves and are good in salads or stir-fries.

CLUSTER TYPE	FLOWER TYPE	LEAF TYPE	LEAF ATTACHMENT
Round	**Irregular**	**Simple**	**Opposite**

Caterpillars
Phacelia congesta

Family: Waterleaf (Hydrophyllaceae)

Height: 6–36" (15–91 cm)

Flower: tightly coiled, hairy spike cluster, 2" (2.5 cm) long, of densely packed, bluish-purple flowers; each flower, ½" (1 cm) wide, appears regular but is actually bell-shaped, with 5 rounded petals around protruding bluish purple-and-yellow flower parts; flowers turn blue when wilted

Leaf: sticky, soft fern-like leaves, 2–4" (2.5–10 cm) long, are deeply cut into 2–7 finely hairy, irregularly toothed lobes

Bloom: early spring, early summer

Cycle/Origin: annual, biennial; native

Habitat: prairies, along streams, roadsides, fences, sun

Range: central, southern, and far western Texas

Notes: Named Caterpillars for the resemblance of the coiled spikes of green flower buds to butterfly larvae. Also known as Blue Curls for the coiled flower clusters, which uncurl as the flowers bloom from the bottom up on the spike. There are more than a dozen similar species in the Phacelia genus in Texas. Plants belonging to this genus are easily identified by the tightly coiled flower spikes and protruding flower parts (stamens). The deeply lobed, hairy leaves are eaten by deer, quail, and turkeys. Also occurs in Oklahoma and New Mexico.

CLUSTER TYPE
Spike

FLOWER TYPE
Bell

LEAF TYPE
Simple Lobed

LEAF ATTACHMENT
Alternate

207

Texas Toadflax
Nuttallanthus texanus

Family: Snapdragon (Scrophulariaceae)

Height: 6–28" (15–71 cm)

Flower: loose spike clusters, 2½" (6 cm) long, of 10–12 pale-lavender flowers; each blossom, ½" (1 cm) long, on a short stalk, has a 2–lobed upper petal (lip) and a 3–lobed horizontal lower lip with a conspicuous, downward-curving spur

Leaf: few slender, stalkless leaves, ½–1" (1–2.5 cm) long, scattered along the upright, slender, flowering stalk; slightly broader leaves are oppositely attached or whorled (forming a rosette) on the long prostrate stems at base of stalk

Bloom: early spring, early summer

Cycle/Origin: annual, biennial; native

Habitat: dry, sandy soils; disturbed sites, abandoned fields, open woods, along roads and railroads

Range: throughout

Notes: Toadflaxes are easily identified by their long spurs, which contain nectar that attracts pollinating insects, and are often referred to as spurred snapdragons. The genus name is for Thomas Nuttall, premier naturalist of the early 1800s. Widespread across much of the United States and frequently seen in wildflower gardens, where the pretty, delicate flowers attract bees and butterflies. Caterpillars of buckeye butterflies eat the foliage.

CLUSTER TYPE
Spike

FLOWER TYPE
Irregular

LEAF TYPE
Simple

LEAF ATTACHMENT
Alternate

LEAF ATTACHMENT
Basal

Horrid Thistle
Cirsium horridulum

Family: Aster (Asteraceae)

Height: 2–5' (61–152 cm)

Flower: reddish-purple flower head (can be dull yellow or white), 2–3" (5–7.5 cm) wide, disk-shaped, made of thin tubular disk flowers; flower head atop base of very slim, extremely spiny bracts

Leaf: narrow, long, elliptical, or lance-shaped leaves, 8–24" (20–61 cm) long, divided into many sharp-spined lobes; basal leaves are in a rosette; stem leaves alternately clasp the stem; very short, thick, white-haired stem has few branches

Bloom: early spring, summer

Cycle/Origin: annual, biennial; native

Habitat: sandy or gravelly soils, open sites, disturbed ground

Range: coastal and eastern Texas, ranging over a third of the state

Notes: Horrid Thistle is common in eastern Texas and near the coast, while Texas Thistle (pg. 115), which has much slimmer stems and narrower leaves, is more common in central, southern, and western Texas. Butterflies love to drink the thistle nectar, and it is timely that thistles bloom just after many butterfly species emerge from their chrysalises. Surprisingly, the miniscule flower parts (anthers) actually move when touched by an insect, curving toward the intruder and covering it with pollen.

FLOWER TYPE
Composite

LEAF TYPE
Simple Lobed

LEAF ATTACHMENT
Alternate

LEAF ATTACHMENT
Clasping

LEAF ATTACHMENT
Basal

Dotted Blazing Star
Liatris punctata

Family: Aster (Asteraceae)

Height: 6–16" (15–40 cm)

Flower: pink-to-purple spike cluster, 2–5" (5–13 cm) long, of densely packed flower heads at top of the stem; each small flower head is composed of 3–7 disk flowers only, with protruding thread-like flower parts

Leaf: stiffly upright, narrow leaves, 2–6" (5–15 cm) long, rough to the touch, are crowded along and spiral up stem, getting smaller toward top of flower spike

Bloom: late summer, fall

Cycle/Origin: perennial; native

Habitat: sandy or limestone soils, prairies, plains, on dry slopes, open hillsides, along roads

Range: throughout Texas, except the northeastern corner of the state

Notes: A native prairie wildflower found throughout the short grass plains of the Midwest and north into Canada. Blooms in late summer and fall, rising above the surrounding grasses. "Dotted" and punctata are for the barely visible, translucent resin dots on the leaves. Also called Gayfeather for the feathery appearance given to the flower spikes by the protruding flower parts. Containing the starch inulin, which can't be metabolized by humans, the mashed roots were used as a mild liver and kidney tonic by Plains Indian tribes. Inulin is now used in a laboratory test of kidney function.

CLUSTER TYPE
Spike

FLOWER TYPE
Composite

LEAF TYPE
Simple

LEAF ATTACHMENT
Alternate

Sanguine Purple Coneflower
Echinacea sanguinea

Family: Aster (Asteraceae)

Height: 1½–4' (45–122 cm)

Flower: large purple or pink flower heads, 3" (7.5 cm) wide, each with 10–20 long slender petals (ray flowers) drooping from the dark blood-red-and-green center made up of disk flowers and sharp scales; single flower head atop 1 to several unbranched stems

Leaf: elliptical or lance-shaped leaves, 4–10" (10–25 cm) long, are rough-haired; lower leaves on stalks mostly near base; stalkless smaller upper leaves alternate along purplish-green stems

Bloom: late spring, early summer

Cycle/Origin: perennial; native

Habitat: dry acidic, sandy, or gravelly soils; hillsides, prairies

Range: eastern and coastal Texas

Notes: A popular plant for herbal remedies, as the roots contain echinacea, which is also used in medical drugs. Genus name comes from the Greek echinos for "spiny" and refers to its dry spiny seed heads. This tall slender wildflower has blood-red disk flowers that turn black with age, thus the species name sanguinea for "blood." Its leaves and stems are usually rough to the touch because of the stiff hairs covering the plant. Found only in Texas and limited areas of Oklahoma, Arkansas, and Louisiana, this cold-sensitive perennial occurs farther south than any other coneflower in the United States.

FLOWER TYPE
Composite

LEAF TYPE
Simple Lobed

LEAF ATTACHMENT
Alternate

LEAF ATTACHMENT
Basal

Western Wild Petunia
Ruellia occidentalis

Family: Acanthus (Acanthaceae)

Height: 12–36" (30–91 cm)

Flower: lavender-to-purple blooms, 3" (7.5 cm) long, are trumpet-shaped; each has 5 petals fused into a long tube, spreading widely at mouth into 2 upper and 3 lower rounded lobes; several upright flowers loosely clustered on flower stalks

Leaf: oval leaves, 1–3" (2.5–7.5 cm) long, have slightly wavy edges; leaves and leafstalks are fuzzy; leaves oppositely attached to very fuzzy white stem

Bloom: summer

Cycle/Origin: perennial; native

Habitat: woods, chaparral, flats, partial to full shade

Range: southern Texas

Notes: Although the blooms resemble garden petunias, this wildflower is a member of the Acanthus family and is not a petunia. The familiar garden petunias belong instead to the Nightshade family. Leaves of wild petunias are eaten by deer and the seeds by quail. Hummingbirds are attracted to the nectar, so this showy wildflower is often cultivated. Western Wild Petunia was once classified as a variety of an important medicinal plant in the Caribbean called Minnieroot (*R. tuberosa*), which is used to treat bladder and kidney disease and to relieve joint and muscle pain. The leaves contain compounds that may reduce inflammation and moderate autoimmune reactions. Foliage is eaten by the caterpillars of Common Buckeye and White Peacock butterflies.

FLOWER TYPE   LEAF TYPE   LEAF ATTACHMENT
Tube   **Simple** **Opposite**

bracts

American Basketflower

Centaurea americana

Family: Aster (Asteraceae)

Height: 3–5' (.9–1.5 m)

Flower: ragged, pale-lavender-and-white (sometimes pink) flower heads, 3–4" (7.5–10 cm) wide, each made up solely of filament-like disk flowers around a white center; layers of stiff comb-like bracts look like a basket holding the flower head; 1 bloom atop each branch

Leaf: stalkless, rough, narrow; leaves, 4–8" (10–20 cm) long, with smooth or shallow-toothed edges; lower leaves larger and more numerous than upper leaves

Bloom: summer

Cycle/Origin: annual; native

Habitat: disturbed soils, prairies, abandoned pastures

Range: throughout

Notes: An annual that is native to the south-central United States and northeastern Mexico. The flower head is made up of thread-like disk flowers that open upright and droop with age. "Basket" in the common name refers to the straw-colored (sometimes prickly) bracts below the flower (see inset). These bracts hold the flower as would a basket and also have a basket weave pattern. The blooms look much like a thistle flower, but the stems of this abundant and widespread wildflower lack thorns. Easily cultivated, these long-lasting cut flowers can be enjoyed fresh or dried to use in bouquets.

FLOWER TYPE **Composite**   LEAF TYPE **Simple**   LEAF ATTACHMENT **Alternate**

Baldwin Ironweed
Vernonia baldwinii

Family: Aster (Asteraceae)

Height: 2–5' (61–152 cm)

Flower: loose, irregular, flat cluster; 3–5" (7.5–13 cm) wide, of 18–34 purple-to-magenta flower heads; each flower head, 1" (2.5 cm) wide, has 15–30 tiny tubular disk flowers only and protruding purple flower parts

Leaf: lance-shaped leaves, 3–6" (7.5–15 cm) long, are sharply toothed and rough above with soft white hairs below; many stalkless or short-stalked leaves are on the stout and hairy, purplish-green stem

Bloom: summer, fall

Cycle/Origin: perennial; native

Habitat: overgrazed ranges, prairies, abandoned fields, along roads and railroads, low areas, partial to full sun

Range: eastern, central, and northwestern Texas

Notes: "Iron" refers to the rust-colored dried flower heads and reddish brown seeds, which resemble the color of rusted iron. Drought- and cold-tolerant, this tall plant looks attractive planted behind other flowers in gardens and is a good choice for butterfly gardens. Readily self-seeds, so remove the faded flower heads if you don't want it to spread. American Indians used ironweed root to make a tea to relieve menstrual cramps. Livestock avoid the bitter-tasting foliage, enabling the plant to invade and overrun large areas. Named for an early 1800s botanist, William Baldwin. Also called Western Ironweed.

CLUSTER TYPE	FLOWER TYPE	LEAF TYPE	LEAF ATTACHMENT
Flat	**Composite**	**Simple**	**Alternate**

Texas Vervain
Verbena halei

Family: Verbena (Verbenaceae)

Height: 12–30" (30–76 cm)

Flower: loose or dense, long and thin spike cluster, 10–15" (25–38 cm) long, of purple or white flowers; each tubular flower, ½" (1 cm) long, is made up of 5 fused petals flaring widely into 2 upper and 3 lower lobes

Leaf: variable leaves, ¾–4" (2–10 cm) long; lower leaves often with deep, narrow toothed lobes, smaller upper leaves with toothed or smooth margins; leaves lack leafstalks and appear to (but don't actually) clasp the square stem that branches at the top

Bloom: any season, except when very cold in winter

Cycle/Origin: perennial; native

Habitat: disturbed areas, rocky slopes, open woods, fields, prairies, roadsides

Range: throughout, except the northwestern part of Texas

Notes: Texas Vervain is a tall, slender plant with a single (or multiple), pencil-thin flower spike that blooms from the bottom up. Its stems are square with oppositely attached leaves, which is why it is often confused with a member of the Mint family. Genus name Verbena is Latin for "sacred plant." In ancient times, the plant was thought to have medicinal properties. The arrangement of the flower lobes resembles a gingerbread man–often said of blossoms in this genus. Attracts butterflies and bees. Sparrows love the seeds.

CLUSTER TYPE
Spike

FLOWER TYPE
Tube

LEAF TYPE
Simple

LEAF TYPE
Simple Lobed

LEAF ATTACHMENT
Opposite

fruit

Wax Mallow

Malvaviscus arboreus

Family: Mallow (Malvaceae)

Height: 3–4' (0.9–1.2 m)

Flower: bright-red flower, ¾–1½" (2–4 cm) long, has 5 broad petals twisted around each other (never unfurling) and long, protruding red flower parts (stamens)

Leaf: broad velvety leaves, 3–5" (7.5–13 cm) long, have 3 shallow lobes, heart-shaped bases, round-toothed margins, and long stalks; upright, woody, widely branched stems

Fruit: apple-shaped green capsule, 1" (2.5 cm) long, turns red

Bloom: spring, summer, fall

Cycle/Origin: perennial; native

Habitat: partly shaded damp areas on hills, woodland edges, along creeks

Range: central, southeastern, and coastal Texas

Notes: "Wax" in the common name is for the waxy appearance of the red petals. Sometimes called Turk's Cap for the resemblance of the closed blossom to a Turkish turban. The large amount of sweet flower nectar attracts butterflies and hummingbirds. Flowers and fruit are edible, and the flower yields a red dye. This abundant, shrubby perennial is frequently cultivated in gardens in the South. Prune in early spring, as only the new growth sprouts flowers.

FLOWER TYPE
Regular

LEAF TYPE
Simple Lobed

LEAF ATTACHMENT
Alternate

FRUIT
Pod

Cardinal Catchfly
Silene laciniata

Family: Pink (Caryophyllaceae)

Height: 12–27" (30–69 cm)

Flower: vivid red flowers, 1–1½" (2.5–4 cm) wide, have 5 deeply fringed petals; each bloom emerges from a tubular, ridged, hairy red calyx, ¾" (2 cm) long

Leaf: lance- to spoon-shaped leaves, ½–6" (1–15 cm) long, are sticky and hairy; a few upper pairs of widely spaced, narrower, and slightly shorter leaves

Fruit: cylindrical to egg-shaped tan capsule, ½" (1 cm) long, with reddish-brown seeds

Bloom: summer, fall

Cycle/Origin: perennial; native

Habitat: rich soils, shaded slopes, mountainsides

Range: far western Texas

Notes: Widely cultivated in the Southwest and southern Midwest for its showy, serrated flowers, this long-blooming plant is easily grown from seed. If planted in early spring, it will bloom the same summer. Its nectar contains about 75% sucrose and is ideal for attracting hummingbirds, which pollinate the plant. Many members of the genus Silene are collectively referred to as catchflies, as the foliage is sticky enough to trap insects. In the wild, found in the Big Bend area in the far western corner of Texas and is common there along hiking trails. Ranges west to southern California and south into Mexico.

FLOWER TYPE **Regular**   LEAF TYPE **Simple**   LEAF ATTACHMENT **Opposite**   FRUIT **Pod**

227

fruit

Red Columbine
Aquilegia canadensis

Family: Buttercup (Ranunculaceae)

Height: 1–4' (30–122 cm)

Flower: orangish red-and-yellow flower, 1–2" (2.5–5 cm) long, made up of a group of 5 upside-down tubes that form a yellow-tipped bell containing nectar-filled spurs

Leaf: compound leaves, 4–6" (10–15 cm) long, made up of 9–27 thin, light-green leaflets; each leaflet has 3 bluntly toothed lobes; leaves on long leafstalks

Fruit: pod-like green container, turns brown and papery with age; 1¼" (3 cm) long, has shiny round seeds

Bloom: spring, summer

Cycle/Origin: perennial; native

Habitat: limestone crevices, steep cliffs

Range: north-central Texas

Notes: One of only two native columbines in Texas, but a cultivated columbine will sometimes escape into the wild. Children often mistake Red Columbine for honeysuckle and bite off its long spurs to suck out the nectar. Its nectar tubes make it a favorite flower of hummingbirds and long-tongued moths. Some insects chew holes in its tubes, cheating to get a little nectar. Genus name Aquilegia is Latin for "eagle." Once considered for our national wildflower because its flower resembles the talons of the Bald Eagle. Grows well in moist, partially shaded gardens, but don't dig up from the wild—plant only seeds.

FLOWER TYPE
Bell

LEAF TYPE
Compound

LEAF ATTACHMENT
Alternate

FRUIT
Pod

229

Devil's Bouquet
Nyctaginia capitata

Family: Four O'clock (Nyctaginaceae)

Height: 12–18" (30–45 cm)

Flower: mounded or flat cluster, 1½–3" (4–7.5 cm) wide, made of 5–20 scarlet-red or reddish-orange flowers; each trumpet-shaped bloom, 1" (2.5 cm) long, has 5 petal-like sepals fused at the base and flaring at the mouth, a green throat, and long protruding red flower parts; blooms have a strong musky odor

Leaf: fuzzy, dull-green leaves, 1½–5" (4–13 cm) long, are teardrop-shaped with rounded bases, pointed tips, and smooth or wavy edges; sticky, hairy, reddish-green stem

Bloom: spring, summer, fall; after rain

Cycle/Origin: perennial; native

Habitat: dry, sandy limestone soils; grasslands, hillsides, fields, roadsides

Range: southern and western Texas

Notes: This upright or sprawling perennial has a single stem spreading from the base in low branches. Colorful, musky-smelling blooms give rise to another common name, Scarlet Muskflower. However, butterflies visiting the blossoms for the nectar don't seem to mind the odor. Deer and livestock avoid the hairy stems and leaves, which are covered with sticky glands. Devil's Bouquet occurs only in Texas, New Mexico, and northern Mexico.

CLUSTER TYPE	FLOWER TYPE	LEAF TYPE	LEAF ATTACHMENT
Flat	**Tube**	**Simple**	**Opposite**

Tropical Sage
Salvia coccinea

Family: Mint (Lamiaceae)

Height: 12–36" (30–91 cm)

Flower: loose spike cluster, 2–9" (5–23 cm) long, of groups of 2–6 scarlet flowers; each bloom, 1" (2.5 cm) long, has 5 fused petals forming a long tube (corolla), smaller arched upper and broader 3–lobed lower petals (lips), and protruding yellow flower parts

Leaf: heart-shaped crinkled leaves, 1–3" (2.5–7.5 cm) long, with blunt-toothed edges; upper leaves are somewhat smaller

Fruit: reddish-brown pod, ½" (1 cm) long, contains 4 dark-brown nutlets

Bloom: early spring, summer, fall

Cycle/Origin: perennial; native

Habitat: sandy soils, chaparral, thickets, pinewoods edges

Range: southern Texas and the eastern half of the state

Notes: This bright wildflower was first discovered in Florida, then cultivated in England as early as the 1700s–it has been a favorite of gardeners ever since. Can be grown in shade as well as sun. Sprouts many stems from a woody base and forms a vase-shaped clump. Short-lived, it reseeds profusely. Blooms during the hottest summer months when other flowering plants may suffer from the heat. Attracts hummingbirds and large butterflies, but deer avoid it due to its pungent aroma. Also called Texas or Blood Sage or Scarlet Salvia.

CLUSTER TYPE
Spike

FLOWER TYPE
Irregular

LEAF TYPE
Simple

LEAF ATTACHMENT
Opposite

FRUIT
Pod

Red Prickly Poppy

Argemone sanguinea

Family: Poppy (Papaveraceae)

Height: 1½–4' (45–122 cm)

Flower: slightly cupped, dull red-to-rose-pink flowers with yellow centers; each flower, 3" (7.5 cm) wide, has 4–6 wrinkled, paper-thin, overlapping petals

Leaf: lance-shaped, bluish-green leaves, 2–6" (5–15 cm) long, with wide, bright bluish-white veins and spiny edges, alternate along the thick stem; lower leaves are deeply lobed

Fruit: narrow or broadly elliptical green pod, 1–1½" (2.5–4 cm) long, covered with spines of unequal length, turns brown and has many tiny dark seeds

Bloom: spring, summer

Cycle/Origin: annual, perennial, biennial; native

Habitat: disturbed areas, pastures, fields, prairies, sun

Range: southern Texas

Notes: This poppy is found only in Texas in the United States, but it ranges south into Mexico. A very prickly plant—the leaf lobes are tipped with spines, there are spines along the leaf veins, the stem is spiny, and the flower buds have long thorns. Because of the prickles, livestock will leave this plant untouched even when there is little else to eat. The seeds are eaten by bobwhite, quail, and doves. However, the orange stem sap is poisonous. A dye has been extracted from the flowers, which are also often used in flower arrangements.

FLOWER TYPE
Regular

LEAF TYPE
Simple

LEAF TYPE
Simple Lobed

LEAF ATTACHMENT
Alternate

FRUIT
Pod

Texas Betony
Stachys coccinea

Family: Mint (Lamiaceae)

Height: 12–30" (30–76 cm)

Flower: scarlet-red spike cluster, 6–18" (15–45 cm) long, of spaced whorls of 3–6 tubular flowers; each bloom, ¾–1½" (2–4 cm) long, has 2 petals (lips), with an upright upper and dangling broad-lobed lower lip

Leaf: oval, dark-green leaves, 3" (7.5 cm) long, are fuzzy, veined, and toothed with pointed tips; evergreen at lower elevations, turning red in cold temperatures; square stems are covered with soft, white hairs

Bloom: spring, summer, fall

Cycle/Origin: perennial; native

Habitat: rich soils, moist crevices of steep slopes, rocky canyons, partial shade

Range: western Texas, especially in the mountains west of the Pecos River

Notes: This showy wildflower requires moist soil and partial shade to thrive in the wild in Texas. Easily grown from seeds or cuttings and blooming for months, it provides gorgeous color and attracts hummingbirds to its nectar. Often cultivated next to partially shaded birdbaths and garden fountains. Said to be disliked by deer and is not often grazed upon. Like others in the Mint family, it has hairy, square stems; two-lipped tubular flowers; and a minty fragrance. Sometimes called Scarlet Hedge-nettle or Scarlet Sage.

CLUSTER TYPE	FLOWER TYPE	LEAF TYPE	LEAF ATTACHMENT
Spike	**Irregular**	**Simple**	**Opposite**

Scarlet Beardtongue
Penstemon murrayanus

Family: Snapdragon (Scrophulariaceae)

Height: 24–36" (61–91 cm)

Flower: spike cluster, 8–12" (20–30 cm) long, of pairs of scarlet-red flowers; each narrow tubular bloom, 1–2" (2.5–5 cm) long, has 5 uneven-size lobes at the mouth

Leaf: blue-green leaves, ½–4" (1–10 cm) long, are downy with smooth edges and surround the red stem; lower leaves are oblong with pointed tips, smaller upper leaves are round and cupped

Bloom: spring, early summer

Cycle/Origin: perennial; native

Habitat: acidic soils, prairies, pinewoods, Post Oak savannahs, meadows, sun

Range: eastern Texas

Notes: One of a group of beardtongues with narrow tubular flowers that accommodate the needle-like bills of hummingbirds. The bright red of the flower is the color most attractive to hummingbirds. There are more than a dozen species of penstemon in Texas, many of which hybridize, making them difficult to distinguish from one another. Scarlet Beardtongue occurs in the wild only in eastern Texas and adjacent parts of Oklahoma, Arkansas, and Louisiana, but it is commonly cultivated in hummingbird and wildflower gardens.

CLUSTER TYPE **Spike**　FLOWER TYPE **Tube**　LEAF TYPE **Simple**　LEAF ATTACHMENT **Opposite**　LEAF ATTACHMENT **Perfoliate**

Scarlet Gilia
Ipomopsis aggregata

Family: Phlox (Polemoniaceae)

Height: 16–30" (40–76 cm)

Flower: orangish-red spike clusters, 10–24" (25–61 cm) long, of slim trumpet-shaped flowers, 1½" (4 cm) long; each bloom is red- or yellow-spotted inside, dangles from stem, and has 5 long, pointed petals that widely flare backward and long, protruding flower parts

Leaf: mostly basal, whitish-green leaves, 1–2" (2.5–5 cm) long, are feather-like, woolly, and divided into 9–11 short thin lobes

Bloom: early spring, summer, late fall

Cycle/Origin: annual, biennial; native

Habitat: sunny to partially shaded dry slopes, upper elevations, brushy areas, open woods

Range: far western and northwestern Texas

Notes: The species name aggregata is Latin for "brought together," referring to the flowers clustering on the unbranched, upright, mostly leafless stems. The eye-catching odorless blooms are pollinated by hummingbirds. The leaves smell skunk-like when crushed. A basal rosette of leaves persists through the winter its first year and withers before blooming in its second summer. Also called Skyrocket, it is frequently cultivated from seed. Eight other species in this genus in Texas, with red, white, or purple flowers.

CLUSTER TYPE
Spike

FLOWER TYPE
Tube

LEAF TYPE
Simple Lobed

LEAF ATTACHMENT
Basal

Cardinalflower
Lobelia cardinalis

Family: Bellflower (Campanulaceae)

Height: 2–4' (61–122 cm)

Flower: tall, open spike cluster; 12–24" (30–61 cm) long, of scarlet-red flowers; each flower, 1½" (4 cm) wide, has 2 upper and 3 spreading lower petals that form a thin tube at its base; flowers alternate on the stem; lower flowers open before upper

Leaf: thin lance-shaped leaves, 2–6" (5–15 cm) long, with toothed margins and pointed tips; purplish-green stem contains a milky sap

Bloom: summer, fall, winter

Cycle/Origin: perennial; native

Habitat: rich, moist soils; near streams and lakes, meadows, wet ditches along roads

Range: throughout

Notes: By far one of the most spectacular wildflowers of Texas, Cardinalflower is found growing in small patches along streams and rivers. Can be grown in backyard oases near water. Its roots need to be wet, and its flowers must have partial shade as well as some sunlight. Not very successful at reproducing, perhaps because it can be pollinated only by hummingbirds. "Cardinal" refers to Roman Catholic cardinals, whose bright-red robes resemble the scarlet-red color of the flowers. Occasionally produces white or rose-colored blooms. All parts of the plant are poisonous.

CLUSTER TYPE	FLOWER TYPE	LEAF TYPE	LEAF ATTACHMENT
Spike	**Irregular**	**Simple**	**Alternate**

Whitemargin Sandmat

Chamaesyce albomarginata

Family: Spurge (Euphorbiaceae)

Height: 8–16" (20–40 cm)

Flower: appears like a single flower, ⅛–¼" (.3–.6 cm) wide, but is actually a tiny, cup-shaped flower cluster; each bloom has 4 petal-like white bracts, each with a maroon pad at the base, around protruding pink and green flower parts

Leaf: round or oblong, smooth, soft, small green leaves, ⅜" (.9 cm) long; sprawling stems have milky sap

Bloom: spring, summer, fall

Cycle/Origin: perennial; native

Habitat: dry soils, deserts, prairies, woodlands, thickets

Range: western two-thirds of Texas

Notes: Some flowers in the Spurge family have colored petal-like bracts, not actual petals. The Christmas Poinsettia is a good example of this, with its red petal-like bracts. The tiny blooms of the widespread Whitemargin Sandmat are actually flower clusters with white bracts, but they look like single flowers. A pair of leaves and the associated flower cluster together measure less than the diameter of a penny. Although the blossoms are tiny, the plant is difficult to miss since one finds it underfoot everywhere, covering the ground in wide sprawling mats usually less than 1 inch (2.5 cm) tall. This plant is also known as Rattlesnakeweed.

FLOWER TYPE LEAF TYPE LEAF ATTACHMENT
Irregular **Simple** **Opposite**

245

Herb of Grace
Bacopa monnieri

Family: Snapdragon (Scrophulariaceae)

Height: 4–12" (10–30 cm)

Flower: solitary white-to-pale-lavender or blue flower, ½" (1 cm) wide, made up of 4–5 unequal-size and shallowly lobed petals

Leaf: succulent oblong leaves, ¾" (2 cm) long, stalkless with smooth edges

Bloom: spring, summer, fall

Cycle/Origin: perennial; native

Habitat: damp or wet soils, roadside ditches, edges of lakes, ponds, marshes, or streams

Range: southern, central, eastern, and coastal Texas

Notes: A creeping perennial with many branches that root where the leaves attach (nodes), forming mats of vegetation. Scientific studies on rats indicate this plant improves memory and learning. Medical investigations have shown it increases the retention of newly learned information in humans and reduces anxiety. Also known as Brahmi in India, where it is used in Ayurvedic medicine (a system of natural medicine) as a treatment for epilepsy and asthma. A popular aquarium plant, it is easily propagated from cuttings. Used to decorate garden ponds and as a ground cover. Sometimes called Smooth Water Hyssop.

FLOWER TYPE | LEAF TYPE | LEAF ATTACHMENT
Regular | **Simple** | **Opposite**

Carolina Geranium
Geranium carolinianum

Family: Geranium (Geraniaceae)

Height: 6–20" (15–50 cm)

Flower: pinkish-white flower, ½" (1 cm) wide, is made up of 5 pink-veined notched petals; hairy, pointed green bracts cup the flower; flowers occur in pairs

Leaf: oval to nearly round leaves, 3" (7.5 cm) wide, are divided into 3–7 deep lobes as wide as they are long; each lobe in turn is divided into lobes with toothed margins; leaves are on long leafstalks

Fruit: narrow, pointed green capsule; turning brown, 1" (2.5 cm) long, shaped like a crane's bill; splits open when ripe, peeling back to show black seeds at base of "beak"

Bloom: early spring, early summer

Cycle/Origin: annual, biennial; native

Habitat: dry to moist soils, fields, open woods, prairies, meadows, roadsides

Range: throughout, but especially the eastern half of Texas

Notes: A weedy plant commonly found wherever the soil has been disturbed. Often overlooked despite its lovely but small flowers. Prefers to grow in sunny spots. Also called Carolina Crane's Bill for the peculiar shape of its seed capsule. Surprisingly, the common houseplant geranium is not in the Geranium genus, but actually is a member of the South African genus Pelargonium.

FLOWER TYPE
Regular

LEAF TYPE
Simple Lobed

LEAF ATTACHMENT
Alternate

FRUIT
Pod

Spiny Aster

Chloracantha spinosa

Family: Aster (Asteraceae)

Height: 2–6' (.6–1.8 m)

Flower: daisy-like white flower head, ½" (1 cm) wide, has 10–30 slender petals (ray flowers) surrounding a button-like yellow center (disk flowers); 1 to several blossoms atop each of the many branches

Leaf: slim lower leaves, ½–2" (1–5 cm) long, wilt and are shed early in the year; upper leaves are scale-like; sharp thorns on lower parts of stems

Bloom: summer, fall, early winter

Cycle/Origin: perennial; native

Habitat: moist soils, seeps, ditches, along streams and rivers, lowlands

Range: throughout

Notes: A tall, spindly wildflower found throughout the Southwest and east to Louisiana, in much of Mexico, and even farther south to Costa Rica. The many-branched Spiny Aster spends most of the year leafless, with thorny, bright-green stems topped by white and yellow blooms. Stout green thorns are usually found low on the stems. Also known as Spiny Goldenbush or Mexican Devilweed. Historically, the young stems were roasted and eaten during famine, but more often were chewed as a sort of gum. Takes over heavily grazed pastures on the plain near the coast.

FLOWER TYPE   LEAF TYPE   LEAF ATTACHMENT
Composite   **Simple**   **Alternate**

Crow Poison

Nothoscordum bivalve

Family: Lily (Liliaceae)

Height: 8–16" (20–40 cm)

Flower: star-shaped white flowers, ½–1" (1–2.5 cm) wide; each has 6 similar-looking oval, pointed sepals and petals (outer ones sometimes with green, red, or purplish-red midline stripe below) surrounding a yellow center; loosely grouped 6–12 fragrant blooms on stalks branching from top of hollow stem

Leaf: 1–4 grass-like basal leaves, 4–15" (10–38 cm) long and only ¼" (.6 cm) wide, have smooth edges and shallow grooves on upper surface

Bloom: early spring, sometimes again in fall

Cycle/Origin: perennial; native

Habitat: lawns, meadows, open woods, prairies, along roads

Range: throughout, but mostly in the eastern two-thirds of the state

Notes: Genus name Nothoscordum means "false garlic," referring to the bulb from which it grows. This onion-like small lily lacks any onion or garlic odor. The species name bivalve means "two-parted" and refers to the tiny fruit, which actually has three parts to its capsule, unlike the two-parted capsule of onion and garlic species in the genus Allium. An abundant spring wildflower after good winter rains, but often overlooked.

FLOWER TYPE
Regular

LEAF TYPE
Simple

LEAF ATTACHMENT
Basal

253

Southern Annual Aster

Symphyotrichum divaricatum

Family: Aster (Asteraceae)

Height: 12–36" (30–91 cm)

Flower: white (sometimes lavender) flower head, turning dark pink, ½–1" (1–2.5 cm) wide, made up of 15–30 petals (ray flowers) around a yellow center (disk flowers); center turns bronzy purple when pollinated; flower heads grow at ends of many short, branching flower stalks

Leaf: narrowly oval leaves, 1–3" (2.5–7.5 cm) long, are stalkless; leaves are larger near the base with upper leaves smaller, reducing to bract-like size on upper zigzag stems

Bloom: late summer, fall

Cycle/Origin: annual, biennial; native

Habitat: moist soils, prairies, stream banks, pond edges, sun

Range: throughout

Notes: Although small, the numerous white flowers on many branching flower stalks make this wildflower noticeable, especially when growing in masses along highways. The flowers are visited by butterflies. Also known as Lawn American Aster for its weedy habit of growing in well-watered lawns. Tolerant of saline soils, so sometimes referred to as Salt Marsh Aster. Found mostly in the southern states from New Mexico east to Alabama and North Carolina, but also ranges as far north as Missouri and Nebraska.

FLOWER TYPE **Composite**   LEAF TYPE **Simple**   LEAF ATTACHMENT **Alternate**

Plains Fleabane
Erigeron modestus

Family: Aster (Asteraceae)

Height: 4–16" (10–40 cm)

Flower: daisy-like white flower head (can be pink or lavender), ¾" (2 cm) wide, made up of layers of 24–65 overlapping narrow petals (ray flowers) striped pink underneath and surrounding a flat yellow center (disk flowers)

Leaf: spoon-shaped basal leaves, 1–2" (2.5–5 cm) long, with a couple of pairs of teeth on the edges; upper stem leaves are smaller

Bloom: early spring, summer, fall

Cycle/Origin: perennial; native

Habitat: dry, rocky limestone soils; openings in thickets, prairies, among junipers or oaks, sun

Range: northwestern and central Texas

Notes: Common in the Southwest, this modest little wildflower ranges west to Arizona and north to Kansas. The form of the plant depends on the season—in early spring, it has a leafless upright stalk with toothed leaves at the base and solitary flowers, but by fall it becomes trailing with many blossoms topping a multi-branched stem and has smaller, narrow leaves with smooth edges. "Fleabane" in the common name is from the belief that the dried plants repelled fleas. Also called Prairie Fleabane.

FLOWER TYPE
Composite

LEAF TYPE
Simple

LEAF ATTACHMENT
Alternate

LEAF ATTACHMENT
Basal

Arkansas Doze Daisy

Aphanostephus skirrhobasis

Family: Aster (Asteraceae)

Height: 6–20" (15–50 cm)

Flower: bright-white flower heads, each ¾–1½" (2–4 cm) wide, made up of 20–40 petals (ray flowers) with pinkish-purple streaks below, around a vivid yellow center (disk flowers); many flowers per plant

Leaf: variable leaves, but usually stalkless, narrowly spoon-shaped, and grayish green; 1–4" (2.5–10 cm) long, hairy with smooth, toothed, or lobed edges; upper leaves are smaller and oblong; single stem branches at the top

Bloom: early spring, summer, fall

Cycle/Origin: annual; native

Habitat: sandy soils, prairies, woodland edges, disturbed ground, along roads, coastal dunes

Range: throughout Texas, except the far western part of the state

Notes: One of the most abundant wildflowers in sandy prairies. Arkansas Doze Daisy is an upright or sprawling, many-branched annual with a solitary white blossom atop each leafy branch. These cheery blooms do not open until noon, thus "Doze" in the common name. The bases of the petals become swollen and harden with age. Cultivated for its drought- and salt-tolerant properties and because it attracts butterflies.

FLOWER TYPE
Composite

LEAF TYPE
Simple

LEAF ATTACHMENT
Alternate

Philadelphia Fleabane
Erigeron philadelphicus

Family: Aster (Asteraceae)

Height: 8–32" (20–80 cm)

Flower: daisy-like, white or pink flower head, 1" (2.5 cm) wide, of layers of 150–250 overlapping narrow petals (ray flowers) surrounding a yellow center (disk flowers); 3–35 blooms top branches arising from the top of stem

Leaf: spoon-shaped basal leaves, 1–4½" (2.5–11 cm) long, are stalkless with coarse-toothed edges; clasping lance-shaped stem leaves, with those on upper stems smaller

Bloom: late winter, spring, summer

Cycle/Origin: perennial, biennial; native

Habitat: moist soils, fields, along roads and railroads, open woods, disturbed areas

Range: central and eastern Texas

Notes: One of the showiest of more than a dozen fleabane species in Texas. Fleabanes are difficult to differentiate from one another due to individual variations in color, size, and season of bloom. However, they are easily distinguished from other asters by the many narrow, overlapping ray flowers. Philadelphia Fleabane has the most numerous petals of all the fleabanes, and clasping stem leaves also help identify this species. American Indians once brewed the plant into a tea that was used as a diuretic and to treat kidney stones.

FLOWER TYPE
Composite

LEAF TYPE
Simple

LEAF ATTACHMENT
Alternate

LEAF ATTACHMENT
Clasping

LEAF ATTACHMENT
Basal

White Clover
Trifolium repens

Family: Pea or Bean (Fabaceae)

Height: 4–10" (10–25 cm)

Flower: round cluster, 1" (2.5 cm) wide, of 40–100 tiny pea-like white flowers tinged with pink; each flower is only ¼" (.6 cm) wide; fragrant cluster is found above the leaves on a single long stalk

Leaf: compound leaves, 1½" (4 cm) wide, composed of 3 round leaflets; each leaflet, ¼–½" (.6–1 cm) wide, has a characteristic crescent- or V-shaped, dusty-white marking and is finely toothed; leaves on stalks

Bloom: spring, summer

Cycle/Origin: perennial; nonnative

Habitat: moist clay or silt soils, fields, lawns, pastures, roadsides, sun

Range: eastern half of Texas

Notes: Well known for occasionally producing a four-leaf clover, White Clover is a Eurasian import that has found a home in lawns across North America. It spreads by an aboveground stem that roots at each leaf attachment (node). The genus name Trifolium describes its three leaflets, while the species name repens refers to its creeping growth habit. Look for the crescent- or V-shaped dusty-white markings on its leaves to help identify this sometimes "lucky" plant. White Clover attracts a number of butterfly species, including skippers, blues, sulphurs, and hairstreaks.

CLUSTER TYPE
Round

FLOWER TYPE
Irregular

LEAF TYPE
Compound

LEAF ATTACHMENT
Alternate

Tenpetal Thimbleweed
Anemone berlandieri

Family: Buttercup (Ranunculaceae)

Height: 5–16" (13–40 cm)

Flower: white or pinkish-blue flowers, 1½" (4 cm) wide; each bloom lacks petals, but has 10–20 elliptical petal-like sepals around a fuzzy green center; single flower tops each upright, long, hairy flower stalk

Leaf: kidney-shaped basal leaves, 1½" (4 cm) wide, are on long stalks and divided into 3 stalkless lobed leaflets with toothed margins; 3 smaller leaves are in a whorl at midstem

Bloom: late winter, spring

Cycle/Origin: perennial; native

Habitat: limestone soils of prairies, on rocky slopes, edges of woodlands

Range: throughout, but especially the central part of Texas

Notes: Although it often goes unnoticed, this very early spring wildflower has fairly large blossoms. It is the most common and widespread anemone in the state, particularly in the hills of central Texas and near the coast. The brown seed head, ½–1" (1–2.5 cm) long, is cone-like, woolly, and produces tiny seed-like fruits that are dispersed by the wind, thus it is sometimes called Windflower Anemone. Tenpetal Thimbleweed grows in the southern United States, ranging from Texas north to Kansas, northeast to Virginia, and east to Florida.

FLOWER TYPE
Regular

LEAF TYPE
Compound

LEAF ATTACHMENT
Whorl

LEAF ATTACHMENT
Basal

Prairie Bluet
Stenaria nigricans

Family: Madder (Rubiaceae)

Height: 4–20" (10–50 cm)

Flower: flat cluster, 1½" (4 cm) wide, of many dainty white or pale-pink flowers; each bloom, ½" (1 cm) long, has 4 fuzzy, pointed, oval petals (sometimes with a dark-pink triangular spot at their bases); loose clusters top the stiff branches of the upper stem and each stalk sprouting from the leaf junctions

Leaf: very narrow, thread-like leaves, ½–1½" (1–4 cm) long; stalkless, with rolled edges and pointed tips; a few smaller leaves are at the leaf junctions

Bloom: summer, fall

Cycle/Origin: perennial; native

Habitat: limestone rock ledges, woodland openings and edges, rocky outcrops

Range: throughout

Notes: A compact, densely branched perennial that has countless leaves and produces abundant clusters of many tiny flowers. These delicate-looking blooms can be white, pale pink, or lavender. Despite its fragile appearance, Prairie Bluet has a deep taproot that enables it to tolerate drought. Also known as Fineleaf Bluet or Diamondflowers for the narrow leaves and pointed petals. The species name nigricans means "black," referring to the color of the leaves when dry.

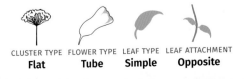

CLUSTER TYPE	FLOWER TYPE	LEAF TYPE	LEAF ATTACHMENT
Flat	**Tube**	**Simple**	**Opposite**

Blackfoot Daisy
Melampodium leucanthum

Family: Aster (Asteraceae)

Height: 5–16" (13–40 cm)

Flower: white flower head, 1–1½" (2.5–4 cm) wide, made up of 8–13 oval petals (ray flowers) with notched blunt tips around a yellow center (disk flowers); single flower head per stalk; many flower heads per plant

Leaf: grayish-green leaves, ¾–1½" (2–4 cm) long, lance-shaped or narrowly oblong, have smooth margins or are sometimes divided into 2–6 shallow lobes; leaves oppositely attached to multi-branched stem

Bloom: summer, fall

Cycle/Origin: perennial; native

Habitat: dry limestone soils, deserts, prairies, along roads, slopes

Range: central and western Texas

Notes: Cultivated in gardens and for erosion control in arid regions because of its hardiness and drought-tolerance, this mounded evergreen perennial has many honey-scented flower heads per plant. Its long taproot allows it to reach water deep underground. "Black" in the common name is for the color the flower parts turn with age, and "foot" describes the developing seed, which looks like a black foot at the base of the yellow center. These seeds are food for birds in fall and winter.

FLOWER TYPE
Composite

LEAF TYPE
Simple

LEAF TYPE
Simple Lobed

LEAF ATTACHMENT
Opposite

Puffballs

Marshallia caespitosa

Family: Aster (Asteraceae)

Height: 6–18" (15–45 cm)

Flower: ragged, round, white flower heads, 1–1½"
(2.5–4 cm) wide, each made up of densely packed,
tiny disk flowers only (lacking ray flowers) with
curled, thread-like, white flower parts (stigmas)
and pinkish-purple flower parts (anthers); single
blossom atop each leafless flower stalk

Leaf: thick, narrow leaves, 2–6" (5–15 cm) long, stalkless
with smooth margins, crowded in a rosette at base

Bloom: spring, summer

Cycle/Origin: perennial; native

Habitat: sandy soils, limestone outcrops, abandoned rangelands, prairies, rocky slopes, edges of woods, full
sun to partial shade

Range: central, eastern and coastal Texas

Notes: A fragrant native prairie wildflower ranging from Texas
north to Kansas and Missouri and east to Louisiana. Spends
the winter as a green rosette of leaves, sending up several
unbranched stems in the spring. The species name caespitosa
describes a plant having a densely clumped growth form, with
the flowers held above the clump. Also called Barbara's Buttons
for the button-like flower heads.

FLOWER TYPE
Composite

LEAF TYPE
Simple

LEAF ATTACHMENT
Basal

Texas Frogfruit
Phyla nodiflora

Family: Verbena (Verbenaceae)

Height: 6–12" (15–30 cm)

Flower: white, round cluster, 1–1½" (2.5–4 cm) wide, has a dark-purple center ringed by small white-to-pink flowers with 5 notched petals; blooms from the bottom up, elongating and looking more like a spike cluster as the flowers below wilt and the upper flowers open

Leaf: thick stalkless leaves, 1–2" (2.5–5 cm) long, dusty green to reddish green with toothed wavy edges; square stem is swollen where leaves attach (nodes)

Bloom: spring, summer, fall

Cycle/Origin: perennial; native

Habitat: disturbed sites, prairies, woodlands, roadsides

Range: scattered throughout Texas, except the northwestern part of the state

Notes: A low, creeping perennial that roots at the leaf nodes where they touch the ground, forming dense mats. Useful as a ground cover in lawns and gardens and along walkways, tolerating dry to wet conditions in full sun to partial shade. The foliage is food for the caterpillars of Common Buckeye, White Peacock, and Phaon Crescent butterflies. The flower nectar attracts adult butterflies. Found throughout the southern two-thirds of the United States, ranging south through Central and South America.

CLUSTER TYPE
Round

FLOWER TYPE
Irregular

LEAF TYPE
Simple

LEAF ATTACHMENT
Opposite

Field Bindweed

Convolvulus arvensis

Family: Morning Glory (Convolvulaceae)

Height: 1–6' (0.3–1.8 m); vine

Flower: funnel-shaped, white or pinkish-white flower, 1–2" (2.5–5 cm) wide, has 5 petals fused together

Leaf: triangular or arrowhead-shaped, dark-green leaves, 1–4" (2.5–10 cm) long, with smooth margins; leaves alternate along 1 side of the climbing, twisting stem

Bloom: spring, summer, fall

Cycle/Origin: perennial; nonnative, from Eurasia

Habitat: old agricultural fields, along roads, usually creeps along the ground, occasionally climbs on fences or shrubs, sun

Range: throughout, but mainly the northern half of Texas

Notes: Field Bindweed seems to prefer disturbed soils, cultivated fields, abandoned lots in cities, and suburban lawns. Grows in large tangled mats, with white flowers that are sometimes slightly pink. This very invasive weed is difficult to eradicate due to its extensive network of roots and underground stems, which can grow as deep as 20 feet (6.1 m), and its seeds, which can live in the soil for as long as 50 years before germinating. Genus name Convolvulus comes from the Latin convolvere, or "to entwine," which accurately describes its growing habit. Lacking tendrils to grasp other plants, it twists its stems around host plants for support, seeking sunlight, a habit that provides its other common name, Possession Vine.

FLOWER TYPE
Tube

LEAF TYPE
Simple

LEAF ATTACHMENT
Alternate

Bastard Toadflax
Comandra umbellata

Family: Sandalwood (Santalaceae)

Height: 6–16" (15–40 cm)

Flower: compact flat cluster, 1–2" (2.5–5 cm) wide, of 3–6 flowers; each star-shaped flower, ⅜" (.9 cm) wide, is greenish white to pinkish white, made of 4–6 petal-like sepals around a greenish-yellow center

Leaf: many stalkless fleshy leaves, ¾–1½" (2–4 cm) wide, are narrowly oval, grayish green above and pale green below; multi-branched stem

Bloom: spring, summer

Cycle/Origin: perennial; native

Habitat: openings in woods, fields, roadsides, rock crevices

Range: northwestern Texas and scattered in the north-central part of the state

Notes: A semiparasitic plant, obtaining some of its nutrients from the roots of other plants. Its green leaves also use the sun to make some of its own food (photosynthesis). Forms colonies along horizontal underground roots, called rhizomes. The greenish-white flowers lack petals, instead displaying petal-like sepals. "Toad" has been used in common plant names to describe any plant that grows in the shade, but it also may come from the word "tod," which is a clump or tuft. Either explanation certainly describes the flowering habit of this plant.

CLUSTER TYPE **Flat** FLOWER TYPE **Regular** LEAF TYPE **Simple** LEAF ATTACHMENT **Alternate**

White Snakeroot
Ageratina altissima

Family: Aster (Asteraceae)

Height: 1–5' (30–152 cm)

Flower: white, flat cluster, 1–2" (2.5–5 cm) wide, made up of numerous tiny, fuzzy flowers; several clusters are on branched stems

Leaf: broadly oval, dark-green leaves, 2–6" (5–15 cm) long, are widest at leaf bases, have pointed tips and edges with ragged teeth

Bloom: late summer, fall

Cycle/Origin: perennial; native

Habitat: moist soils, stream banks, shady disturbed sites

Range: southeastern third of Texas

Notes: Well known as a late-summer and fall bloomer, White Snakeroot often grows along the shady edges of woods. Contains a toxic chemical that, if ingested by a cow, causes milk sickness. If humans then drink milk produced by that cow, they will also contract the disease, which is the very same sickness suggested to have killed Abraham Lincoln's mother. Today, because of better food availability for cows and modern processing, this is no longer a health concern. Many plants share "Snake" in their common names because of the belief that a plant growing in shade harbors snakes or because it may be used for snakebite treatment. Like some other Aster family members, this plant has composite flowers made up entirely of disk flowers, lacking ray flowers.

CLUSTER TYPE **Flat**   FLOWER TYPE **Composite**   LEAF TYPE **Simple**   LEAF ATTACHMENT **Opposite**

White Milkwort
Polygala alba

Family: Milkwort (Polygalaceae)

Height: 8–15" (20–38 cm)

Flower: slender spike cluster, 1–3" (2.5–7.5 cm) long, narrowing at the top, of densely packed, tiny white flowers with yellow centers; cluster tops a leafless flower stalk

Leaf: narrowly lance-shaped or thread-like leaves, ¼–1" (0.6–2.5 cm) long; basal leaves in 2–3 whorls; narrower upper stem leaves are alternate

Bloom: spring, summer, fall

Cycle/Origin: perennial; native

Habitat: sandy or rocky dry soils, prairies, hillsides, ravines, mesquite thickets, among cedars

Range: western, central, and coastal Texas, ranging over three-quarters of the state

Notes: The most widespread of all the milkworts in Texas, as well as the Great Plains of the United States and Canada. Has as many as two dozen stems branching from the base. Although it often grows among taller grasses, it is conspicuous due to its white flowers. Polygala means "much milk," for the mistaken belief that cows eating plants in this genus would produce more milk. Species name alba is Latin for "white." American Indians used the roots of White Milkwort to treat earaches. First described in 1818 by the great English botanist Thomas Nuttall.

CLUSTER TYPE
Spike

FLOWER TYPE
Irregular

LEAF TYPE
Simple

LEAF ATTACHMENT
Alternate

LEAF ATTACHMENT
Basal

Woolly Plantain
Plantago patagonica

Family: Plantain (Plantaginaceae)

Height: 4–10" (10–25 cm)

Flower: hairy, greenish-white spike cluster, 1–5" (2.5–13 cm) long, of tiny crowded flowers interspersed with white-haired, pointed green bracts; each blossom has 4 translucent white-to-tan petals around a red center; 1–20 flower spikes per plant

Leaf: hairy, long, narrow, basal leaves, 1–6" (2.5–15 cm) long, with pointed tips

Bloom: early spring, late summer

Cycle/Origin: annual; native

Habitat: prairies, woodlands, along roads, mesas, slopes

Range: central and western Texas, ranging over two-thirds of the state

Notes: Although the flowers of Woolly Plantain are inconspicuous, the flower spikes of this common small annual are noticeable when they grow in masses along highways. The whole plant is densely covered with woolly white hairs, but it looks green from a distance. American Indians curbed their appetites with a tea brewed from the plant and used it to treat headaches and diarrhea. It is sometimes called Indian Wheat because the seeds were once harvested for food. The seeds are also eaten by birds and small rodents. This plant is widespread across the United States.

CLUSTER TYPE
Spike

FLOWER TYPE
Regular

LEAF TYPE
Simple

LEAF ATTACHMENT
Basal

Snow on the Mountain
Euphorbia marginata

Family: Spurge (Euphorbiaceae)

Height: 12–36" (30–91 cm)

Flower: flat clusters, 2–3" (5–7.5 cm) wide, of 5–7 tiny, cup-shaped, white-and-green flowers; clusters are surrounded by dense whorls of leaf-like green bracts with broad white edges

Leaf: oval, stalkless, dull-green leaves, 1–3" (2.5–7.5 cm) long; lower leaves alternate, upper leaves opposite; stems and leaves ooze milky sap when broken or cut

Bloom: summer, fall

Cycle/Origin: annual; native

Habitat: dry, disturbed limestone soils; fields, prairies

Range: northwestern, western, central, and southern Texas

Notes: Species name marginata is for the showy white edges of the green bracts below the flowers. Petal-like colored bracts are sometimes found in Spurge family members—a good example is the Christmas Poinsettia, which doesn't have true flowers, but has petal-like red bracts. "Spurge" is from the Latin word meaning "to purge," describing the laxative properties of plants in the family. The milky sap is corrosive to the skin, causing burns or rash. Some early cattlemen used the sap for branding cattle instead of a hot branding iron. Often cultivated as an ornamental, but be careful where you plant it, as it can be invasive. Can survive cold winters with an average temperature of -10°F (-23°C), but needs summer days with high heat.

CLUSTER TYPE
Flat

FLOWER TYPE
Irregular

LEAF TYPE
Simple

LEAF ATTACHMENT
Alternate

LEAF ATTACHMENT
Opposite

Common Yarrow
Achillea millefolium

Family: Aster (Asteraceae)

Height: 12–36" (30–91 cm)

Flower: flat cluster, 2–4" (5–10 cm) wide, of 5–20 densely packed, white (sometimes pink) flower heads; each small flower head has 4–6 (usually 5) petals surrounding a tiny center

Leaf: fern-like, finely divided, feathery leaves, 4–6" (10–15 cm) long, have a strong aroma and become progressively smaller toward the top of the hairy stem; stalked lower and stalkless upper leaves

Bloom: spring, summer, sometimes fall

Cycle/Origin: perennial; native

Habitat: disturbed sites, woodland and thicket edges, old fields, along roads

Range: throughout

Notes: A common wildflower of open fields and along roads. A native of Eurasia as well as North America, it is uncertain which of our plants were introduced or are native. Often confused with a type of fern because of its leaves. Grows in large clusters due to a horizontal underground stem (rhizome). The genus name Achillea comes from the Greek legend that Achilles used the plant to treat bleeding wounds during the Trojan War. Species name millefolium means "thousand leaves," referring to the many divisions of the leaf, making one leaf look like many.

CLUSTER TYPE
Flat

FLOWER TYPE
Composite

LEAF TYPE
Simple Lobed

LEAF ATTACHMENT
Alternate

fruit

Red Whisker Clammyweed
Polanisia dodecandra

Family: Caper (Capparaceae)

Height: 12–36" (30–91 cm)

Flower: elongated flower clusters, 2–6" (5–15 cm) long, of frilly, pinkish-white flowers; each bloom, ¾" (2 cm) wide, has 4 clawed petals notched at tips and many protruding pinkish-purple flower parts

Leaf: stalked, dark-green leaves, 2½–4" (6–10 cm) long, are clammy to the touch and divided into 3 fine-haired elliptical leaflets; upper leaves are smaller

Fruit: bean-like, reddish-green pod, 1–3" (2.5–7.5 cm) long, is upright, flattened, and fuzzy; turns tan

Bloom: year-round

Cycle/Origin: annual; native

Habitat: sandy and open disturbed areas, pastures, deserts, thickets, beaches, along roads, sun

Range: throughout

Notes: The foliage of this sticky-haired annual has a rank, resinous odor and so many glands on its surface that it feels chilly and moist, thus "Clammyweed" in the common name. The species name dodecandra means "having 12 stamens" in Latin, referring to the long and obvious flower parts. Often cultivated for the scentless, airy flowers and because this plant self-sows readily, filling in empty spots in the garden. Grows best in full sun. Found throughout the United States and most of Canada.

CLUSTER TYPE
Round

FLOWER TYPE
Irregular

LEAF TYPE
Palmate

LEAF ATTACHMENT
Alternate

FRUIT
Pod

White Waterlily

Nymphaea odorata

Family: Waterlily (Nymphaeaceae)

Height: aquatic

Flower: floating white flowers, 3–6" (7.5–15 cm) wide, each made up of many pointed petals surrounding a yellow center

Leaf: round or heart-shaped leaves, 5–12" (13–30 cm) wide, have smooth edges and are shiny, deeply notched, and float on the water

Bloom: spring, summer, fall

Cycle/Origin: perennial; native

Habitat: roadside ditches, streams, ponds

Range: eastern half of Texas

Notes: Also called Fragrant Waterlily. The leaves float directly on the surface of still water and sometimes are referred to as lily pads. This common pond lily requires quiet water, rooting to bottoms of ponds and small lakes. Roots produce large tubers that are often eaten by muskrats. Its stems and leaves have air channels that trap air to keep the plant afloat. The flowers open on sunny days, closing at night and on cloudy days.

FLOWER TYPE **Regular** LEAF TYPE **Simple** LEAF ATTACHMENT **Basal**

Spring Lady's Tresses
Spiranthes vernalis

Family: Orchid (Orchidaceae)

Height: 8–25" (20–64 cm)

Flower: creamy white spike cluster, 3–6" (7.5–15 cm) long, with as many as 50 fragrant fuzzy flowers in a single spiral twisting around the sticky, softly hairy flower stalk; each slightly drooping, fleshy bloom, ½" (1 cm) long, is held by a pointed green bract

Leaf: narrow, lance-shaped basal leaves, 2–8" (5–20 cm) long, sharply pointed, with bases closely clasping the stem; smaller upper leaves; 4–5 leaves per stem

Bloom: spring, summer

Cycle/Origin: perennial; native

Habitat: dry to moist soils, prairies, old fields, cemeteries

Range: eastern Texas

Notes: "Lady's Tresses" is for the shape of the flower spike, which resembles braided hair. Also called Twisted Lady's Tresses. Genus name Spiranthes is derived from a Greek word meaning "spiral," and species name vernalis means "spring." The tallest and earliest-flowering orchid in Texas. Also the most common and weediest of all native orchids, Spring Lady's Tresses readily forms large colonies, and hundreds to thousands of plants can be seen lining roadside ditches or covering prairies. The basal leaves are usually present when the plant flowers, unlike many other species in the genus.

LUSTER TYPE	FLOWER TYPE	LEAF TYPE	LEAF ATTACHMENT	LEAF ATTACHMENT	LEAF ATTACHMENT
Spike	**Irregular**	**Simple**	**Alternate**	**Clasping**	**Basal**

Evening Rain Lily
Cooperia drummondii

Family: Lily (Liliaceae)

Height: 6–18" (15–45 cm)

Flower: large white flower, 3–7" (7.5–18 cm) long, has translucent petals fused at base into a long, slender tube, flaring widely into 6 slightly cupped, pointed lobes around a pale-yellow throat; single bloom held by a conspicuous red bract atop leafless flower stalk

Leaf: grayish-green basal leaves, 10–12" (25–30 cm) long, are grass-like and elongate after the flower wilts

Fruit: 3–celled, reddish-green capsule, 1" (2.5 cm) wide, turns brown and contains shiny black seeds

Bloom: year-round, except when very cold in winter

Cycle/Origin: perennial; native

Habitat: prairies, lawns, savannahs, woodland edges, full sun

Range: throughout

Notes: Aptly named, these fragrant flowers appear quickly after heavy rains, open in the evening, and stay open for 2–4 days before fading. Blooms most abundantly in late summer and autumn, but can flower almost any month of the year. The glossy seeds are eaten by quail and other birds. Grows from bulbs, which can be divided to propagate this wildflower anytime, or from seeds planted in the fall. Genus name Cooperia is in honor of James Graham Cooper, a geologist and physician who was the first to study Elf Owls and Desert Tortoises.

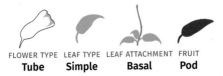

FLOWER TYPE **Tube**   LEAF TYPE **Simple**   LEAF ATTACHMENT **Basal**   FRUIT **Pod**

fruit

Bluestem Prickly Poppy

Argemone albiflora

Family: Poppy (Papaveraceae)

Height: 1½–5' (45–152 cm)

Flower: slightly cupped white flowers with yellowish-orange centers; each flower, 4" (10 cm) wide, has 6 wrinkled, paper-thin, overlapping petals

Leaf: lance-shaped, bluish-green leaves, 3–8" (7.5–20 cm) long, partly or deeply lobed with wavy spiny edges; upper leaves clasp the spiny stem

Fruit: green pod, 1–1½" (2.5–4 cm) long, covered with spines of unequal length, turns brown and has many tiny dark seeds

Bloom: spring, summer, fall

Cycle/Origin: annual, biennial; native

Habitat: disturbed areas, overgrazed land, abandoned fields, along roads

Range: eastern, central, and southern Texas

Notes: Growing abundantly in overgrazed or otherwise disturbed soils, such as along highways, this is the most common poppy in Texas. The entire plant is poisonous due to the numerous toxic alkaloids it contains, although Mourning Doves do eat the seeds. The stem sap is white, turning yellow when exposed to air. However, the flowers are fragrant and attract bees and moths, which seek the abundant pollen. Interestingly, butterflies usually do not visit this wildflower since it contains little nectar.

FLOWER TYPE
Regular

LEAF TYPE
Simple Lobed

LEAF ATTACHMENT
Alternate

LEAF ATTACHMENT
Clasping

FRUIT
Pod

fruit

Texas Bullnettle
Cnidoscolus texanus

Family: Spurge (Euphorbiaceae)

Height: 18–36" (45–91 cm)

Flower: flat cluster, 4–5" (10–13 cm) wide, of white flowers, 1" (2.5 cm) wide; each bloom lacks petals, but has 5 widely flaring, petal-like sepals fused into a tube

Leaf: white-dotted, bright-green leaves, 3–6" (7.5–15 cm) long, on long stalks and deeply divided into 3–5 toothed lobes; long needle-like hairs that sting when touched cover the leaves and stems; hollow stems contain milky sap

Fruit: 6-parted green capsule, turning brown, has long hairs and contains 3 edible seeds

Bloom: spring, summer, fall

Cycle/Origin: perennial; native

Habitat: dry, sandy disturbed soils; old fields, along roads

Range: throughout, except in parts of western Texas

Notes: Sometimes called Mala Mujer ("bad woman" in Spanish) for the foliage, which is covered with hairs that can irritate skin, producing a stinging sensation lasting a half hour or more, or even cause burns or rashes. Some people are very allergic to the corrosive, milky sap in the stems. With several low, branching stems growing from a single taproot, this weed is tolerant of dry conditions and can spread widely, forming large colonies. The fragrant white flowers attract honeybees, butterflies, and other insects.

CLUSTER TYPE
Flat

FLOWER TYPE
Tube

LEAF TYPE
Simple Lobed

LEAF ATTACHMENT
Alternate

FRUIT
Pod

leaves

Broadleaf Arrowhead
Sagittaria latifolia

Family: Water-plantain (Alismataceae)

Height: aquatic

Flower: white spike cluster, 4–6" (10–15 cm) long, of whorls of 3 flowers; each regular flower, 1½" (4 cm) wide, has 3 paddle-shaped petals around a yellow center; male flowers on upper part and female flowers on lower part of the same flower stalk

Leaf: arrowhead-shaped basal leaves, 4–12" (10–30 cm) long, are smooth-edged, dark green, and on long stalks growing above or below the surface of water

Bloom: summer, fall

Cycle/Origin: perennial; native

Habitat: marshes, swamps, ponds, lakes, calm streams

Range: eastern Texas

Notes: Found throughout the United States and most of Canada, wherever shallow, still water is present. Also called Duck Potato for the tuberous root, which was cooked as one would a potato and eaten by American Indians and by early 1800s explorers Lewis and Clark. Ducks, geese, wading birds, songbirds, muskrats, and beavers eat the tubers and seeds. Often cultivated in colonies by refuge managers because the roots and foliage clean polluted water and buffer the wave action of speedboats, as well as provide cover and food for wildlife. This useful plant is also known as Wapato, an historic American Indian name for the tuber.

CLUSTER TYPE
Spike

FLOWER TYPE
Regular

LEAF TYPE
Simple Lobed

LEAF ATTACHMENT
Basal

Crimsoneyed Rosemallow

Hibiscus moscheutos

Family: Mallow (Malvaceae)

Height: 4–5' (1.2–1.5 m)

Flower: slightly cup-shaped, white or all-pink flower, 4–7" (10–18 cm) wide, has 5 wedge-shaped petals, a magenta center outlined in pink, and white or yellow flower parts; pointed green sepals (calyx)

Leaf: egg- or lance-shaped leaves, 6–8" (15–20 cm) long, are grayish green and smooth above, white with soft hairs below, and have wavy edges and long stems; upper leaves irregularly toothed

Fruit: oval or rounded green capsule, turning reddish brown, 1½" (4 cm) long, is tipped with short "beak" and partly enclosed by persistent brown calyx; contains dark-brown seeds

Bloom: summer, fall

Cycle/Origin: annual, perennial; native

Habitat: wet to well-drained soils, swamps, roadsides

Range: eastern half of Texas

Notes: A many-flowered plant that grows in colonies of more than 200. Although a perennial in the wild, most of the fast-growing varieties have been cultivated as annuals and have flowers as wide as 9–12 inches (22.5–30 cm), ranging from white to dark crimson. Each showy flower lasts only a day, but this is a colorful plant to use for mass plantings, borders, or planting along streams or ponds.

FLOWER TYPE **Regular** LEAF TYPE **Simple** LEAF ATTACHMENT **Alternate** FRUIT **Pod**

Lateflowering Thoroughwort
Eupatorium serotinum

Family: Aster (Asteraceae)

Height: 3–5' (.9–1.5 m)

Flower: flat cluster, 5" (13 cm) wide, made up of hundreds of fuzzy, dull-white flower heads, ¼" (.6 cm) wide; each flower head composed of many disk flowers (no ray flowers); clusters loosely spaced atop branches at the top of stem

Leaf: lance-shaped, gray-green leaves, ¾–3½" (2–9 cm) long, with smooth or coarse-toothed edges and on stalks; the reddish-green stem has lines of small white hairs

Bloom: summer, fall

Cycle/Origin: perennial; native

Habitat: dry or moist soils, overgrazed pastures, along roads and streams, thickets, open woods

Range: eastern and south-central Texas

Notes: Found throughout the eastern US, this is one of more than a dozen similar species of Eupatorium in Texas. The flowers are very popular with many insects, such as bees, wasps, butterflies, and moths. The leaves are bitter and avoided by deer and livestock, but are eaten by caterpillars of Rounded Metalmark butterflies—so named because the adults have shiny silver bands on their wings. Sometimes called Late or False Boneset since it looks like Boneset (*E. perfoliatum;* not shown), which is found in far eastern Texas.

CLUSTER TYPE	FLOWER TYPE	LEAF TYPE	LEAF ATTACHMENT
Flat	**Composite**	**Simple**	**Opposite**

fruit

Sacred Datura
Datura wrightii

Family: Nightshade (Solanaceae)

Height: 1–5' (30–152 cm)

Flower: trumpet-shaped white (sometimes tinged with lavender) flower, 6–8" (15–20 cm) long, has 5 large fused petals with slightly wavy outer ends and a short spike at the middle edge of each petal

Leaf: arrowhead-shaped leaves, 1–10" (2.5–25 cm) long, are dark bluish green and have prominent veins

Fruit: globular prickly green pod, turns brown at maturity, 1½" (4 cm) wide

Bloom: spring, summer, fall

Cycle/Origin: annual, perennial; native

Habitat: disturbed ground, deserts, hills, along roads and washes

Range: throughout

Notes: The fragrant flowers of Sacred Datura, which are pollinated by hawk moths, open in the evening and wither a few hours after sunrise. All parts contain hallucinogenic compounds and are poisonous—just handling the plant can cause skin irritation. One of four poisonous nightshades in the Datura genus in Texas. Daturas were important to American Indians, who used them for medicinal and ritual purposes, thus "Sacred" in the common name. Also called Sacred Thornapple for the seedpod, which resembles a spiny apple.

FLOWER TYPE	LEAF TYPE	LEAF ATTACHMENT	LEAF ATTACHMENT	FRUIT
Tube	**Simple**	**Alternate**	**Opposite**	**Pod**

Spring Spiderlily
Hymenocallis liriosme

Family: Lily (Liliaceae)

Height: 12–36" (30–91 cm)

Flower: fragrant, airy white flowers, 8" (20 cm) wide; each has 6 long, thin petals with 6 flower parts (stamens) joined by a membrane, forming a white cup with a yellow-tinged center; 5–12 blossoms open a few at a time atop the 2–edged leafless stalk

Leaf: 5–8 upright, narrow, flat blades, 12–34" (30–86 cm) long, are bright green and leathery with pointed tips; each leaf has a lengthwise groove

Fruit: egg-shaped, dark-green capsule, 1" (2.5 cm) long

Bloom: spring, early summer

Cycle/Origin: perennial; native

Habitat: wet soils, prairies, meadows, ditches along roads, marshes, along creeks and rivers

Range: southeastern Texas

Notes: When in shade, the spider-like, bright-white flowers atop the leafless stems can appear like ghosts floating in midair. The genus name Hymenocallis, Greek for "beautiful membrane," refers to the white membrane joining the stamens. Gardeners like this plant because deer avoid it, but it is poisonous and has little value to wildlife. Cultivated in wetland gardens, this sweet-smelling flower is best grown in partial shade to full sun and in medium-wet soils that never dry out. Plant bulbs 4 inches (10 cm) deep in soil in the fall.

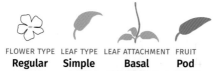

FLOWER TYPE **Regular**   LEAF TYPE **Simple**   LEAF ATTACHMENT **Basal**   FRUIT **Pod**

fruit

Pokeweed

Phytolacca americana

Family: Pokeweed (Phytolaccaceae)

Height: 4–10' (1.2–3 m)

Flower: distinctive spike cluster, 6–10" (15–25 cm) long, with many tiny white, green, or pink flowers; each blossom has no petals, but has 5 petal-like sepals around a green center

Leaf: smooth-edged, oblong leaves, 5–10" (13–25 cm) long, tapering at both ends

Fruit: whitish-green berry, turning dark purple to black when ripe, ½" (1 cm) wide, flattened on each end; in drooping clusters on green (turning red) stems

Bloom: late summer, fall

Cycle/Origin: perennial; native

Habitat: disturbed areas, woodland edges, fencerows

Range: eastern half of Texas

Notes: A large and obvious plant with a history of various uses. Emerging green shoots in spring were once gathered and cooked. However, as the plant matures, its leaves and shoots turn reddish and become toxic. Pokeweed berries (known as pokeberries) are named for the shape of the berry, which looks as if the ends were squeezed or "poked" together. The berries are poisonous to humans and livestock, but are consumed safely by birds. In the 19th century, pokeberry juice was used as a dye and as ink. Many letters were written with "poke" juice during the Civil War.

CLUSTER TYPE
Spike

FLOWER TYPE
Regular

LEAF TYPE
Simple

LEAF ATTACHMENT
Alternate

FRUIT
Berry

White Crownbeard
Verbesina virginica

Family: Aster (Asteraceae)

Height: 3–6' (.9–1.8 m)

Flower: ragged flat cluster, 10–12" (25–30 cm) wide, of white flower heads; each flower head, ¾" (2 cm) wide, has 3–5 petals (ray flowers) unevenly spaced around a green-and-white center (disk flowers)

Leaf: broadly lance-shaped leaves, 4–8" (10–20 cm) long, with shallow-toothed edges, on long leafstalks extending down the stem and forming narrow wings; smaller upper leaves are stalkless

Bloom: late summer, fall

Cycle/Origin: perennial, biennial; native

Habitat: moist soils, roadsides, creek edges, woods, partially shaded areas

Range: central, eastern, and coastal Texas

Notes: White Crownbeard can occur in large dense masses under trees or along streams. Often called Frostweed for the large amount of foamy sap that exudes and freezes when a hard frost splits the winged stems, making interesting ice formations. The dried leaves were once used as a tobacco substitute by American Indians. The foliage is avoided by deer and livestock. Cultivate in shady portions of the garden for the brightening effect of the white blossoms, which attract bees and butterflies.

CLUSTER TYPE	FLOWER TYPE	LEAF TYPE	LEAF ATTACHMENT
Flat	**Composite**	**Simple**	**Alternate**

Dogweed
Thymophylla pentachaeta

Family: Aster (Asteraceae)

Height: 4–8" (10–20 cm)

Flower: small, daisy-like yellow flower head, ½" (1 cm) wide, has 12–21 (usually 13) short oval petals around a wide, orangish-yellow center of many tiny disk flowers; each bloom is well above the leaves on its own nearly leafless stalk

Leaf: stiffly lobed, sticky, slightly fuzzy leaves, 1" (2.5 cm) long, divided into 3–5 (usually 5) thread-like lobes with pointed prickly tips; densely leafy on lower half of the stem only; the plant has many stems

Bloom: year-round

Cycle/Origin: perennial; native

Habitat: dry soils, prairies, deserts, cliffs, roadsides

Range: throughout Texas, except the northeastern corner of the state

Notes: A very common, low-growing perennial that prefers drier soil containing calcium. It is often seen growing along highways. The individual small flower heads are inconspicuous, but a yellow haze appears to float above the ground after heavy rains, when mats of Dogweed bloom. The aromatic leaves are required food for the caterpillars of the tiny Dainty Sulphur butterfly. Also known as Five-needle Pricklyleaf for the needle-like lobes of the leaves.

FLOWER TYPE
Composite

LEAF TYPE
Simple Lobed

LEAF ATTACHMENT
Opposite

315

Broom Snakeweed
Gutierrezia sarothrae

Family: Aster (Asteraceae)

Height: 6–36" (15–91 cm); shrub

Flower: daisy-like yellow flower head, ½" (1 cm) wide, composed of 3–8 slim petals (ray flowers) around a yellowish-orange center (disk flowers); 2–6 flower heads atop each of the upper branches

Leaf: sticky thread-like leaves, ¾–2½" (2–6 cm) long, with pointed tips and smooth edges; leaves alternate on densely branching stem or cluster at leaf junctions

Bloom: summer, fall

Cycle/Origin: perennial; native

Habitat: dry, sandy, or clay soils; disturbed sites, prairies

Range: central, coastal, southern, and western Texas

Notes: Toxic to cattle and sheep, this shrub can be an indication of overgrazed rangelands and is often the first plant to reestablish itself in an area following severe drought. A many-branched perennial that is brown-stemmed below and green above, topped with a layer of yellow blooms. The long taproot allows it to find water deep in the soil. Drought-deciduous when no water is available, it conserves moisture by dropping its leaves and becomes dormant. The dried foliage is extremely flammable, thus other common names, Kindlingweed or Matchweed. Species name sarothrae is derived from the Latin word for "broom." Eaten by Mule Deer and provides nearly a third of the diet of Pronghorn Antelope.

FLOWER TYPE   LEAF TYPE   LEAF ATTACHMENT
Composite   **Simple**   **Alternate**

Prairie Broomweed
Amphiachyris dracunculoides

Family: Aster (Asteraceae)

Height: 16–36" (40–91 cm)

Flower: many yellow flower heads, each ½–¾" (1–2 cm) wide, with 5–15 petals (ray flowers) around a yellow center (disk flowers)

Leaf: narrowly lance-shaped leaves, 1–2½" (2.5–6 cm) long, are sticky; scarce upper leaves are much smaller; single stem branches at the top

Bloom: late summer, fall

Cycle/Origin: annual; native

Habitat: sandy or rocky soils, prairies, thickets, woodland edges, disturbed ground, overgrazed rangelands, along roads

Range: throughout

Notes: Prairie Broomweed is an aromatic, many-branched annual with a solitary yellow bloom atop each branch. A single plant can have as many as 1,500 flowers. Carpets acres of land with yellow in autumn. The plant loses most of the leaves by the time it blooms, exposing the distinctive, wiry, bright-green stems. Livestock avoid this toxic plant, enabling it to overrun drought-stricken or over-grazed rangelands that have little grass. Various opinions exist on the meaning of "Broomweed" in the common name. One theory is that settlers used the dried plant as a broom; another is the weed resembles an upside-down broom head.

FLOWER TYPE **Composite**   LEAF TYPE **Simple**   LEAF ATTACHMENT **Alternate**

fruit

Gordon Bladderpod
Lesquerella gordonii

Family: Mustard (Brassicaceae)

Height: 4–12" (10–30 cm)

Flower: loose groups of bright-yellow flowers; each flower, ¾" (2 cm) wide, has 4 oval petals that are shallowly notched at the tips

Leaf: oblong or lance-shaped, grayish-green basal leaves, ½–3" (1–7.5 cm) long, variable margins; stem leaves are smaller, narrower; stems often lie on the ground

Fruit: nearly spherical, smooth green pod, ⅜" (.9 cm) wide, with a lengthwise brown band and tipped with thread-like projection; turns brown with age

Bloom: spring, summer

Cycle/Origin: annual; native

Habitat: gravelly or sandy soils, pastures, prairies, plains, along washes and roads, hillsides, under shrubs

Range: western half of Texas

Notes: After good winter rains in the desert, Gordon Bladderpod occurs in huge patches on flats among creosote bushes. Eighteen species of bladderpod are in Texas. Named for the partially hollow seedpods that when stepped on make a popping sound—thus they are also referred to as popweeds. The bladderpods belong to the Mustard family, hence the peppery taste of their edible seeds and young leaves. Ranges west to southern Arizona and north to Kansas.

FLOWER TYPE	LEAF TYPE	LEAF TYPE	LEAF ATTACHMENT	LEAF ATTACHMENT	FRUIT
Regular	Simple	Simple Lobed	Alternate	Basal	Pod

Greenleaf Five Eyes
Chamaesaracha coronopus

Family: Nightshade (Solanaceae)

Height: 6–18" (15–45 cm)

Flower: pale greenish-yellow-to-cream, star-shaped flower, ¾" (2 cm) wide, of fused fuzzy sepals and petals held by a globe-shaped green calyx; each petal has a raised yellow or white spot at the base

Leaf: hairy, thick, rough, narrowly lance-shaped leaves, 1–4" (2.5–10 cm) long, have wavy margins

Fruit: berry-like yellow fruit, ¼" (.6 cm) wide, has dark-brown seeds; persistent, 5–lobed, papery calyx

Bloom: spring, summer, fall

Cycle/Origin: perennial; native

Habitat: dry limestone soils, deserts, mesquite woodlands, prairies, abandoned fields, mesas, plains

Range: western two-thirds of Texas

Notes: This low-growing plant is also called Small Groundcherry or Prostrate Groundcherry for its yellow fruit and sprawling stems. The mounded yellow or white spot at the base of each narrow petal gives rise to "Five Eyes" in the common name. Texas has seven flowers in the genus Chamaesaracha that are very similar to Greenleaf Five Eyes.

FLOWER TYPE
Regular

LEAF TYPE
Simple

LEAF ATTACHMENT
Alternate

FRUIT
Berry

Camphorweed
Heterotheca subaxillaris

Family: Aster (Asteraceae)

Height: 12–36" (30–91 cm)

Flower: daisy-like yellow flower head, ½–1" (1–2.5 cm) wide, composed of 15–30 petals (ray flowers) and a yellow-orange center (disk flowers); many flower heads per plant atop the branched upper stem

Leaf: oval leaves, 1–4" (2.5–10 cm) long, have smooth or slightly toothed margins, are stalked and alternate lower on the stem; leaves along middle and upper stem are stalkless and clasping; leaves and the single stem are hairy and sticky due to glands in the hairs

Bloom: year-round

Cycle/Origin: annual, biennial; native

Habitat: sandy soils, along roads, disturbed open sites, prairies, old fields, dunes, woodland edges

Range: throughout

Notes: This sparse- or dense-leaved aster is named for the camphor-like odor emitted from its leaves when crushed. It is very weedy and drought-tolerant. Ranchers dislike it because cows avoid eating it, and the plant can take over pastures. However, it does serve as food for the caterpillars of several moth species. When applied to injuries, such as sprains or bruises, the foliage is said to diminish pain, inflammation, and swelling.

FLOWER TYPE **Composite**   LEAF TYPE **Simple**   LEAF ATTACHMENT **Alternate**   LEAF ATTACHMENT **Clasping**

Fendler Bladderpod

Lesquerella fendleri

Family: Mustard (Brassicaceae)

Height: 4–16" (10–40 cm)

Flower: bright-yellow flower, 1" (2.5 cm) wide, has 4 widely separated petals; blooms occur in loose groups atop stalks

Leaf: hairy, silvery green leaves, 1–3" (2.5–7.5 cm) long, are narrowly elliptical with smooth or toothed edges; stalkless upper leaves, lower leaves are on stalks

Fruit: smooth, round, green pod; ⅜" (.9 cm) wide, matures and turns brown while some flowers are still opening, contains flattened rust-colored seeds

Bloom: early spring, summer; sometimes in fall after rain

Cycle/Origin: perennial; native

Habitat: sandy or rocky soils, disturbed sites, mesas and pastures

Range: western third of Texas

Notes: Clumps of silvery green stems sport groups of golden-yellow flowers in early spring. The seeds have a large amount of oil containing hydroxy fatty acids, an important raw material used in cosmetics, resins, waxes, nylons, plastics, and lubricating greases. This oil may also replace castor oil for some uses in the future since the United States no longer produces that oil—all castor oil is now imported. Fendler Bladderpod seeds contain a complete protein similar to soybeans, so it can be used to feed livestock. The plant is easily cultivated and drought-tolerant.

FLOWER TYPE	LEAF TYPE	LEAF ATTACHMENT	LEAF ATTACHMENT	FRUIT
Regular	**Simple**	**Alternate**	**Basal**	**Pod**

Spreading Fanpetals
Sida abutifolia

Family: Mallow (Malvaceae)

Height: 12–24" (30–61 cm); vine

Flower: dull brownish-yellow flower, 1" (2.5 cm) wide, has 5 fan-shaped petals with notched edges and yellow-to-green bases, around a bright-yellow center; backed by light-green sepals fused into a star shape

Leaf: hairy, dark-green leaves, ½–1" (1–2.5 cm) long, narrowly lance-shaped, folded lengthwise, scalloped red-tinged margins; hairy, reddish-green stems

Fruit: triangular yellow capsule, ¼" (.6 cm) wide, turning tan, contains many tiny seeds

Bloom: spring, summer, fall

Cycle/Origin: annual, perennial; native

Habitat: bare alkaline soils, disturbed areas, deserts, grassy areas, prairies, along roads

Range: southern, central, and far western portions of Texas, ranging over half of the state

Notes: The branched hairs covering the leaves and stems are typical of plants in the Mallow family, as are the fused flower parts (stamens) forming a column in the center. This low-growing herb has become a troublesome invasive weed in some situations such as in irrigated fields. Found in North America, Central America, and Australia, but just where this little flower originated is debated. The leaves are occasionally eaten by White-tailed Deer and cattle.

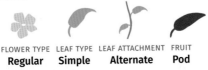

FLOWER TYPE **Regular** LEAF TYPE **Simple** LEAF ATTACHMENT **Alternate** FRUIT **Pod**

Hoary False Goldenaster

Heterotheca canescens

Family: Aster (Asteraceae)

Height: 8–20" (20–50 cm)

Flower: daisy-like yellow flower head, 1" (2.5 cm) wide, composed of 14–20 slim petals (ray flowers) and a yellow center (disk flowers); 1 to several flower heads atop the curved and branching upper stems

Leaf: grayish-green leaves, 1–2" (2.5–5 cm) long, are densely packed, narrow, lance-shaped, and have smooth margins; lower leaves on stalks; upper leaves stalkless, sometimes clasping; leaves and the many stems are softly hairy

Bloom: late spring, summer, fall

Cycle/Origin: perennial; native

Habitat: dry, shallow, sandy soils; roadsides, disturbed open sites, prairies, gravelly slopes, woodland openings

Range: central and northwestern Texas

Notes: This perennial spreads easily and rapidly in exposed areas that are hot and dry. Forms numerous, eye-catching, symmetrical clusters as wide as 12–24 inches (30–61 cm). An abundance of small, bright-yellow flowers found above the silvery green leaves cover the plant from late spring to fall. The leaves frequently have a strong, pleasant aroma. Cherokee Indians drank a tea made from the foliage as a sleeping aid. This goldenaster is found in Texas, New Mexico, Oklahoma, Kansas, and Missouri.

FLOWER TYPE
Composite

LEAF TYPE
Simple

LEAF ATTACHMENT
Alternate

LEAF ATTACHMENT
Clasping

Lacy Tansyaster
Machaeranthera pinnatifida

Family: Aster (Asteraceae)

Height: 8–24" (20–61 cm)

Flower: daisy-like, golden-yellow flower head, 1" (2.5 cm) wide, with 1 to several layers of 30–45 narrow petals (ray flowers) around an orangish-yellow center (disk flowers); clasped below by layers of pointed, bristle-tipped, upright bracts

Leaf: oblong to spoon-shaped, grayish-green leaves, ½–2½" (1–6 cm) long, are stalkless and have pairs of narrow lobes with smooth or toothed margins that are always tipped with bristly hairs; upper leaves tiny; thin, woolly stems; branches are interwoven

Bloom: spring, summer, fall

Cycle/Origin: perennial; native

Habitat: limestone soils, deserts, open areas in woodlands, prairies, rocky hillsides

Range: western third of Texas

Notes: Lacy Tansyaster leaves and flowers are highly variable. Look for the solitary, golden-yellow flowers that appear to float above the upright branches, since the leaves are tiny on the upper stems. "Lacy" in the common name is for the feather-like leaves found on the lower half of the stems. Also called Cutleaf Iron Plant for the lobed leaves and its woody base, which is very hard when dried.

FLOWER TYPE
Composite

LEAF TYPE
Simple

LEAF TYPE
Simple Lobed

LEAF ATTACHMENT
Alternate

Texas Yellowstar
Lindheimera texana

Family: Aster (Asteraceae)

Height: 10–24" (25–61 cm)

Flower: star-shaped yellow flower head, 1" (2.5 cm) wide, has 5 short, oval petals (ray flowers) notched at their tips, around a yellow center (disk flowers); single or several blossoms tip the stems

Leaf: fuzzy, oval leaves, 1–3" (2.5–7.5 cm) long, have pointed tips and wavy or toothed edges; lower leaves are alternate, upper leaves are opposite; stout, hairy stem is unbranched or branching at top and dotted with red spots (glands)

Bloom: spring, early summer

Cycle/Origin: annual; native

Habitat: prairies, full sun

Range: central, northern, and southern Texas

Notes: Oddly for an Aster family member, Texas Yellowstar (the only species in the genus Lindheimera) produces seeds solely from the ray flowers, not the disk flowers. Thus, there is only one fruit per ray flower, resulting in five fruits per flower. After the fruits mature, the plant dies. The scattered seeds germinate in the fall, sprouting a rosette of leaves that grows slowly throughout the winter, awaiting spring to send up its single flowering stem. This kind of plant is known as a winter annual. Texas has lots of winter annual wildflowers, including Sandyland and Texas Bluebonnet (pp. 43 and 53, respectively).

FLOWER TYPE
Regular

LEAF TYPE
Simple

LEAF ATTACHMENT
Alternate

LEAF ATTACHMENT
Opposite

LEAF ATTACHMENT
Basal

Slenderleaf Sneezeweed

Helenium amarum

Family: Aster (Asteraceae)

Height: 8–20" (20–50 cm)

Flower: daisy-like yellow flower head, 1" (2.5 cm) wide, made of 8–10 fan-shaped drooping petals (ray flowers) circling a mounded yellow or brown center (disk flowers); each petal tip is 3–lobed

Leaf: many thread-like leaves, 1–3" (2.5–7.5 cm) long and only ⅒" (.2 cm) wide; sometimes smaller clusters of leaves near each junction (axis) of the larger leaves; hairy stems

Bloom: year-round, except in the coldest winter weather

Cycle/Origin: annual; native

Habitat: dry, sandy, or poor soils; disturbed sites, prairies, old fields, roadsides, along railroads

Range: throughout

Notes: Sometimes called Bitterweed, sharing a common name with the similar and distantly related, but larger-flowered Bitterweed (pg. 391). An aromatic and wide-ranging weed that has spread across the eastern United States and the Midwest. It is frequently found in disturbed or waste areas such as abandoned yards or gravel pits. Contains toxins that make the plant unpalatable to humans and livestock. Cows will graze upon the plant in poor pasture, but then produce tainted, bitter milk. A robust plant with long-blooming flowers and a good choice for cultivation in wildflower meadows.

FLOWER TYPE **Composite** LEAF TYPE **Simple** LEAF ATTACHMENT **Alternate**

Upright Prairie Coneflower
Ratibida columnifera

Family: Aster (Asteraceae)

Height: 12–36" (30–91 cm)

Flower: cylindrical, yellowish-brown cone, 1" (2.5 cm) tall, of hundreds of tiny disk flowers surrounded by 4–12 drooping oval petals (ray flowers) that are yellow, red, or bicolored; 1–15 flower heads per plant, each on a long stalk above the leaves

Leaf: stiff, thin leaves, ¾–6" (2–15 cm) long, have 3–14 long, narrow uneven lobes; are hairy and alternately attached

Bloom: year-round

Cycle/Origin: perennial; native

Habitat: prairies, open areas in pine forests, along roads, grassy areas, disturbed ground, sun

Range: throughout

Notes: In the wild, this drought-tolerant prairie plant is widespread in the Great Plains of the Midwest. Has been used in prairie restorations. A cultivated ornamental often grown in wildflower gardens, it frequently escapes to roadsides and prairie-like habitats. The Cheyenne Indians made a solution from the leaves and stems that was applied to the skin to draw out poison from rattlesnake bites and for relief from Poison Ivy symptoms. Often called Mexican Hat, for the sombrero-like shape of the flower head.

FLOWER TYPE
Composite

LEAF TYPE
Simple Lobed

LEAF ATTACHMENT
Alternate

Resinbush
Viguiera stenoloba

Family: Aster (Asteraceae)

Height: 18–36" (45–91 cm); shrub

Flower: golden-yellow flower heads, 1" (2.5 cm) wide; each has short petals (ray flowers) around a wide, raised, orange center; each bloom held by an upward-curving, pointed, sticky green bract

Leaf: bright-green leaves, 1–2½" (2.5–6 cm) long, are white below, deeply divided into narrow thread-like lobes and stalkless

Bloom: summer, fall

Cycle/Origin: perennial; native

Habitat: dry, rocky soils; prairies, abandoned fields, along roads, rocky slopes, full sun

Range: southern and western Texas

Notes: This rounded evergreen shrub is nearly 3 feet (0.9 m) wide and is native only to Texas, New Mexico, and northern Mexico. Common in the Chihuahuan Desert. Frequently cultivated, it tolerates full sun and dry conditions. The flowers attract butterflies and other insects, but deer avoid the plant due to the aromatic oils in the foliage. The species name stenoloba means "narrow-lobed," referring to the lobed leaves that are so deeply cut they appear to be "mere skeletons of their former selves," and giving rise to another common name, Skeletonleaf Goldeneye. The genus Viguiera was named after Louis Viguier, an early 1800s French botanist.

FLOWER TYPE
Composite

LEAF TYPE
Simple Lobed

LEAF ATTACHMENT
Alternate

Spiny Sowthistle
Sonchus asper

Family: Aster (Asteraceae)

Height: 1–6' (.3–1.8 m)

Flower: dandelion-like yellow flower head, 1" (2.5 cm) wide, made up of slender petals (ray flowers) with fringed tips; many flower heads per plant

Leaf: lance- or spoon-shaped leaves, 2½–6" (6–15 cm) long, are shiny, dark green, and stiff, with very wavy spiny margins and curled rounded bases that clasp the stems; upper leaves much smaller; branching, purplish-green stem contains milky sap

Bloom: year-round

Cycle/Origin: annual; nonnative

Habitat: agricultural areas, disturbed sites, along roads, in old fields

Range: throughout

Notes: Spiny Sowthistle is an introduced plant that has become a very invasive weed, spreading over much of the United States. Like a dandelion, its seeds are dispersed by the wind. Due to its deep taproot and spiny leaves, this stout plant is hard to eradicate. A southern Texas look-alike, Common Sowthistle (*S. oleraceus*; not shown), has leaves that are less spiny than Spiny Sowthistle and a curled leaf base that tapers to a point at the outside of the curl, unlike the ear-shaped leaf base of this plant.

FLOWER TYPE Composite

LEAF TYPE Simple

LEAF TYPE Simple Lobed

LEAF ATTACHMENT Alternate

LEAF ATTACHMENT Clasping

Large Buttercup
Ranunculus macranthus

Family: Buttercup (Ranunculaceae)

Height: 6–36" (15–91 cm)

Flower: butter-colored or orangish-yellow flowers, 1–1½" (2.5–4 cm) wide, each with 10–22 waxy, oval petals in a couple of layers around a wide yellow center of many flower parts

Leaf: variable leaves, but usually compound basal, 1½–4" (4–10 cm) long, on long stalks and divided into 3–7 lobed leaflets; stalkless stem leaves (cauline) with smooth or lobed edges

Bloom: spring, summer

Cycle/Origin: perennial; native

Habitat: moist to wet soils, woodlands, ditches, meadows, along streams, swamps, shade

Range: central and coastal Texas

Notes: This largest and showiest of the buttercups in Texas is more widespread than the more than a dozen other species, but it is limited to where moisture is plentiful. Its upright or sprawling stems are very hairy. The blossoms produce little nectar but much nutritious pollen, thereby attracting pollen-eating beetles, flies, and bees. Large Buttercup is found only in Texas, Arizona, and New Mexico. Most buttercups are poisonous to livestock, and the sap from the foliage can produce a rash on some people.

FLOWER TYPE **Regular** LEAF TYPE **Simple Lobed** LEAF TYPE **Compound** LEAF ATTACHMENT **Alternate** LEAF ATTACHMENT **Clasping** LEAF ATTACHMENT **Basal**

fruit

Partridge Pea
Chamaecrista fasciculata

Family: Pea or Bean (Fabaceae)

Height: 1–5' (30–152 cm)

Flower: yellow flower, 1–1½" (2.5–4 cm) wide, made of 5 teardrop-shaped petals around dark-red flower parts; 4 upper petals have a dark-red base (1 of the outer petals curves back over the center)

Leaf: compound leaves, 2–3" (5–7.5 cm) long, are delicate, feather-like, and made up of 10–15 pairs of small, oval leaflets; leaves alternately attached along the upright reddish-green main stem

Fruit: thin, flat, hairy pod; 1–2½" (2.5–6 cm) long, green, turning brown and containing 10–20 seeds; looks like a common garden pea pod

Bloom: summer, fall

Cycle/Origin: annual; native

Habitat: dry, sandy soils; disturbed areas, open woods, fields

Range: eastern half of Texas

Notes: This Pea family member doesn't have the characteristic pea flowers—its petals are almost equal in size. The leaves fold up in direct sun, hence it is also called Sensitive Pea. Common, it grows in a wide variety of habitats throughout Texas. A host plant for Little Yellow and Cloudless Sulphur butterfly caterpillars. Adult butterflies are drawn to the nectar secreted surprisingly by the small orange glands at each leaf base.

FLOWER TYPE
Irregular

LEAF TYPE
Compound

LEAF ATTACHMENT
Alternate

FRUIT
Pod

Plains Zinnia
Zinnia grandiflora

Family: Aster (Asteraceae)

Height: 4–12" (10–30 cm); shrub

Flower: bright-yellow flower heads, 1–1½" (2.5–4 cm) wide; each has 3–6 round, shallowly notched petals (ray flowers) surrounding a reddish-orange center (disk flowers)

Leaf: narrow leaves, 1–2" (2.5–5 cm) long, are light green, fuzzy, and twisted; densely and oppositely attached along branching stems

Bloom: summer, fall

Cycle/Origin: perennial; native

Habitat: dry limestone soils, deserts, prairies, along roads, hillsides, mesas

Range: northwestern third of Texas

Notes: A perennial shrub forming rounded mounds of foliage nearly completely covered with long-lasting yellow flowers. The flowers dry and persist on the plant into fall, turning papery and brown. Spreads by underground stems (rhizomes) to form large colonies. Also called Rocky Mountain Zinnia, this Aster family member ranges from Texas west to Arizona and north to Kansas. Often cultivated as a showy ground cover and used in borders, as it is drought-tolerant and cold hardy.

FLOWER TYPE **Composite**   LEAF TYPE **Simple**   LEAF ATTACHMENT **Opposite**

349

Awnless Bush Sunflower

Simsia calva

Family: Aster (Asteraceae)

Height: 6–24" (15–61 cm)

Flower: golden-yellow flower head, 1–1½" (2.5–4 cm) wide, has 8–21 separated oval petals (ray flowers) around an orange center (disk flowers); 1–3 blooms atop a long, leafless flower stalk; each blossom backed by pointed hairy bracts

Leaf: sandpapery triangular leaves, ½–1" (1–2.5 cm) long, with edges shallowly lobed; leafstalks are broadly winged and fused at base (perfoliate) around the rough, hairy, stout stem; upper leaves are smaller

Bloom: spring, summer, fall

Cycle/Origin: perennial; native

Habitat: well-drained sandy limestone soils, clay soils with calcium carbonate (caliche), pine-oak woodlands, prairies, thickets, along streams and roads

Range: southern, central, and far western Texas

Notes: A low-growing, ragged-looking, bushy plant that occurs in the wild in the United States only in Texas and New Mexico. Has brittle, woody stems and is very drought-tolerant. Leaves and stems are covered with stiff hairs, making them feel rough to the touch. The winged leafstalks join around the stem to form disks, a characteristic that differentiates it from closely related species and from another similar-looking aster, Camphorweed (pg. 325).

FLOWER TYPE
Composite

LEAF TYPE
Simple Lobed

LEAF ATTACHMENT
Opposite

LEAF ATTACHMENT
Perfoliate

Curlycup Gumweed
Grindelia squarrosa

Family: Aster (Asteraceae)

Height: 12–36" (30–91 cm)

Flower: daisy-like yellow flower head, 1–1½" (2.5–4 cm) wide, with 25–40 short, oval, overlapping petals (ray flowers) around a darker yellow center (disk flowers) atop layers of downward-curving green bracts

Leaf: variable-shaped leaves, oval to spoon-shaped, 1–3" (2.5–7.5 cm) long, have coarse-toothed edges and are dotted with glands; middle and top leaves alternately clasp the multi-branched, reddish-green stem

Bloom: summer, fall

Cycle/Origin: annual, perennial, biennial; native

Habitat: dry, sandy limestone soils; prairies, open areas, overgrazed land, open woods

Range: northwestern, western, and central Texas, ranging over half of the state

Notes: Probably originating in the Great Plains, this aster is very common along roads in Texas. There are two varieties—one has blooms with ray flowers, the other has only disk flowers. A tea made from the leaves and flowers was used by Plains Indian tribes to treat bronchitis. Species name squarrosa and "Curlycup" in the common name both refer to the conspicuous, outward-curving bracts that make this aster unusually easy to identify. The bracts have glands that exude a sticky resin, thus the name "Gumweed."

FLOWER TYPE **Composite**   LEAF TYPE **Simple**   LEAF ATTACHMENT **Alternate**   LEAF ATTACHMENT **Clasping**

Hartweg Sundrops

Calylophus hartwegii

Family: Evening primrose (Onagraceae)

Height: 12–16" (30–40 cm)

Flower: large yellow flower, 1–2½" (2.5–6 cm) wide, fading to pink, made up of 4 wide (nearly square) wrinkled petals; center is same color as the petals

Leaf: narrowly oval, grayish-green leaves, ½–1½" (1–4 cm) long, are basally and alternately attached to stem; sometimes smaller leaves grow at leaf attachments

Fruit: 4–parted, cylindrical, green pod, ¼–1½" (.6–4 cm) long, fuzzy with white hairs, has many tiny seeds

Bloom: spring, summer

Cycle/Origin: perennial; native

Habitat: deserts, prairies, woodlands, hillsides, along roads, plains

Range: western half of Texas

Notes: Hardy and drought-tolerant, this low-growing evergreen plant is often cultivated in rock gardens as ground cover. Its masses of blooms attract hawk moths. The flowers open in the afternoon or near sunset and bloom until the next afternoon, when they are replaced by more buds. American Indians used this plant to treat internal bleeding. Ranges from Texas as far west as Arizona and north to Kansas.

FLOWER TYPE **Regular**   LEAF TYPE **Simple**   LEAF ATTACHMENT **Alternate**   LEAF ATTACHMENT **Basal**   FRUIT **Pod**

Golden Tickseed

Coreopsis tinctoria

Family: Aster (Asteraceae)

Height: 12–36" (30–91 cm)

Flower: golden-yellow flower head, 1¼" (3 cm) wide; usually has 8 slim petals (ray flowers); petals have lobed tips, are often deep red at their bases and surround a brownish-red center (disk flowers)

Leaf: compound leaves, 4" (10 cm) long, divided (sometimes twice) into long, narrow, oblong leaflets with smooth edges; stiff and wiry stem has numerous angled branches

Bloom: spring, summer, fall

Cycle/Origin: annual; native

Habitat: moist or dry soils, abandoned fields, disturbed areas, prairies, ditches

Range: throughout

Notes: Native to the Great Plains from Minnesota south to Texas and Louisiana, this wildflower is now found throughout the United States. A beautiful, cheery blossom that attracts butterflies, it is commonly cultivated in gardens and for use as a cut flower in floral arrangements. Also does well in wildflower meadows, reseeding if the small, slim seeds fall on bare ground. Germinates in early spring or in fall, overwintering as a small rosette of leaves. Tolerates full sun and dry conditions once established. The Texas Department of Transportation seeds Golden Tickseed along highways.

FLOWER TYPE
Composite

LEAF TYPE
Compound

LEAF ATTACHMENT
Opposite

Butterfly Daisy
Amblyolepis setigera

Family: Asteraceae (Aster Family)

Height: 6–15" (15-38 cm)

Flower: two-toned, yellow flower head, 1¼–2" (3–5 cm) wide, has domed velvety centers (disk flowers) that are dark yellow, surrounded by 8–12 paler yellow, overlapping petals (ray flowers) with 3–4 deep notches at tips. Each bloom sits atop a bare stem.

Leaf: alternate, blue-green leaves, 2–4" (5–10 cm) long, can be hairy or smooth; lower leaves are spatula-shaped, wider at tips and attach directly to fuzzy stems, upper smaller leaves are oval and clasp the stems; ascending branches from a single stout, hairy stem, upper stems without leaves

Bloom: spring, summer

Cycle/Origin: annual; native

Habitat: chaparral, disturbed areas, open fields, and roadsides; full sun or partial shade, dry, well-drained soil

Range: the panhandle, central and west Texas

Notes: In the US, this wildflower is only found in Texas, but it ranges south into northeastern Mexico. Attractively erect and an eye-catching gold, this conspicuous bloom forms thick stands along roads and wide swaths sweeping up hillsides. It's commonly called Huiscache Daisy as it regularly grows in the chaparral under the huiscache bush (*Vachellia farnesiana*). Because it is so ornamental and sweetly fragrant, Butterfly Daisy is often seeded in decorative borders and meadows to attract pollinators.

FLOWER TYPE	LEAF TYPE	LEAF ATTACHMENT	LEAF ATTACHMENT
Composite	**Simple**	**Alternate**	**Clasping**

Mexican Primrosewillow
Ludwigia octovalvis

Family: Evening primrose (Onagraceae)

Height: 1–4' (30–122 cm)

Flower: single yellow flower, 1½" (4 cm) wide, with 4 heart-shaped petals around a yellow center; 4 pointed green sepals (calyx) below and between petals; on a short stalk from upper leaf junctions

Leaf: slim, oval leaves, 2–6" (5–15 cm) long, crinkled above; multi-branched, red-tinged stem

Fruit: long, slender red pod, 1–2" (2.5–5 cm) long, turning brown, has 8 ribs; inside of pod is segmented by 8 thin walls or valves; has many rounded black seeds

Bloom: summer, fall

Cycle/Origin: perennial; native

Habitat: wet soils, edges of marshes or ponds, ditches, along streams, disturbed sites

Range: southern and eastern Texas

Notes: Common and widespread in wet areas throughout the southern United States, growing in large colonies. Almost showier in autumn than when blooming—the sepals turn nearly red and remain on the fruit after the petals drop, looking like pink blooms. The attractive slim pods are often included in dried flower bouquets. The species name octovalvis, from Latin words for "eight" and "folding door," refers to the eight valves inside the fruit.

FLOWER TYPE **Regular** LEAF TYPE **Simple** LEAF ATTACHMENT **Alternate** FRUIT **Pod**

Common Dandelion
Taraxacum officinale

Family: Aster (Asteraceae)

Height: 2–18" (5–45 cm)

Flower: appears to be 1 large yellow flower, 1½" (4 cm) wide, but is actually a composite of many tiny flowers that are clustered together

Leaf: rosette of dark-green basal leaves, 2–8" (5–20 cm) long, with deep lobes and sharp teeth

Bloom: year-round

Cycle/Origin: perennial; nonnative

Habitat: disturbed ground, lawns, roadsides, along trails

Range: throughout

Notes: This nonnative perennial is responsible for much water contamination, as people treat lawns with chemicals to eradicate Common Dandelion. In French, dent-de-lion refers to the toothed leaves, which resemble the teeth of a lion. Its flowers open in mornings and close in afternoons. The globe-like seed heads have soft, hair-like bristles that resemble tiny parachutes, which carry the seeds away on the wind. Originally brought from Eurasia as a food crop. Its leaves are bitter but offer high vitamin and mineral content. The long taproot has been roasted and ground to use as a coffee substitute.

FLOWER TYPE
Composite

LEAF TYPE
Simple Lobed

LEAF ATTACHMENT
Basal

Plains Yellow Daisy

Tetraneuris scaposa

Family: Aster (Asteraceae)

Height: 6–18" (15–45 cm)

Flower: solitary flower head, 1½" (4 cm) wide; has 12–31 long, narrow, yellow petals (ray flowers) with 4 dark reddish-brown veins on the undersides and 3–lobed tips, surrounding a yellow center (disk flowers)

Leaf: grayish-green basal leaves, 1–4" (2.5–10 cm) long, are narrow and oval with pointed tips; densely dotted with glands; leaves are sticky and smelly when crushed

Bloom: spring, summer, fall

Cycle/Origin: perennial; native

Habitat: limestone ledges, dry plains, prairies, rocky slopes

Range: western, central, and southern Texas

Notes: Also called Stemmy Four-nerve Daisy for the clumps of many silky-haired stems rising from a woody base and the four dark lines on each petal. Cheery yellow blooms top leafless flower stalks well above the basal rosette of leaves, but the plant lacks leafy stems. Species name scaposa refers to these leafless flower stalks, called scapes by botanists. Sometimes called Plains Bitterweed for its taste and odor. Avoided by deer, it can form mats covering large areas. Ranges from Colorado, Kansas, and Arkansas south into northern Mexico. Drought- and heat-tolerant. Grown in rock gardens and borders for its interesting foliage and long blooming time.

FLOWER TYPE **Composite**   LEAF TYPE **Simple**   LEAF ATTACHMENT **Basal**

Texas Sleepy Daisy
Xanthisma texanum

Family: Aster (Asteraceae)

Height: 8–30" (20–76 cm)

Flower: single yellow flower head, 1½" (4 cm) wide, has 18–22 slender pointed petals (ray flowers) around a yellow center (disk flowers); flower head held by layers of pointed green bracts curving outward

Leaf: stalkless, narrowly oval leaves, 1–2½" (2.5–6 cm) long, with pointed tips; some lower leaves toothed or lobed, smaller upper leaves with smooth margins; upright branches in upper part of single stem

Bloom: any season, except in the coldest winter weather

Cycle/Origin: annual; native

Habitat: dry sandy soils, abandoned fields, rocky slopes

Range: throughout Texas, except the far eastern and western portions of the state

Notes: Native to the prairies of Texas, Oklahoma, and New Mexico. The genus name Xanthisma is Greek for "something dyed yellow," referring to the flowers. One of only a few species in this unique genus. Many people first see the attractive yellow blossoms on long stalks swaying gracefully in the wind along the highway. Frequently cultivated since it is grown easily from seed and blooms 8–10 months of the year. Aptly named "Sleepy" for the flower's habit of not opening until almost noon and closing by late afternoon.

FLOWER TYPE LEAF TYPE LEAF ATTACHMENT
Composite Simple   Alternate

Engelmann Daisy
Engelmannia peristenia

Family: Aster (Asteraceae)

Height: 18–36" (45–91 cm)

Flower: yellow flower head, 1½" (4 cm) wide, composed of 8 petals (ray flowers) around a small yellow center; several flower heads atop the upper branches

Leaf: fern-like basal leaves, 4–12" (10–30 cm) long, are deeply lobed, toothed, coarsely haired, and on long stalks; stalkless leaves have fewer lobes and alternate along the branching upper stem

Bloom: spring, summer, fall

Cycle/Origin: perennial; native

Habitat: dry soils, along roads, prairies, savannahs, pinyon-juniper woodlands, desert scrub

Range: throughout, except the far eastern part of Texas

Notes: Found among native grasses, this drought-tolerant perennial is covered with bright-yellow flowers throughout the warmer months. The pointed-tipped blooms first open widely in the late afternoon, but the next day's heat causes the petal tips to curl under, giving the blooms a rounded appearance. Winters as a basal rosette of deeply divided leaves, thus another common name, Cutleaf Daisy. The only species in the genus Engelmannia, named after 1800s Missouri physician and botanist George Engelmann, who also has several other species bearing his name. Ranges from Texas north through South Dakota and south into Mexico.

FLOWER TYPE
Composite

LEAF TYPE
Simple Lobed

LEAF ATTACHMENT
Alternate

LEAF ATTACHMENT
Basal

Narrowleaf Puccoon

Lithospermum incisum

Family: Forget-me-not (Boraginaceae)

Height: 4–12" (10–30 cm)

Flower: groups of many trumpet-shaped yellow flowers; each tubular flower, 1½" (4 cm) long, has a wide mouth with 5 fringed lobes

Leaf: narrow, hairy, dark-green leaves, 1–4" (2.5–10 cm) long; upper leaves become progressively smaller; 1 to several hairy stems

Bloom: early spring, early summer

Cycle/Origin: perennial; native

Habitat: sandy soils, prairies, fields, woodland openings, along roads

Range: throughout Texas, except the far eastern edge of the state

Notes: Found across the West and Midwest, this hairy and upright plant has single or multiple slender stems topped with abundant yellow tubular flowers. The species name incisum is for the fringed edges of the petals, appearing as if cut. Genus name Lithospermum is from the words for "stone" and "seed," referring to the very hard, ripe nutlets that look like tiny polished stones. These stony nutlets were traditionally eaten by American Indians. A purple dye was extracted from the root. In fact, "Puccoon" in the common name is an American Indian word that refers to plants that yield dyes. The root was also used for medicinal purposes.

FLOWER TYPE
Tube

LEAF TYPE
Simple

LEAF ATTACHMENT
Alternate

fruit

Reverchon Blazing Star

Mentzelia reverchonii

Family: Stickleaf (Loasaceae)

Height: 6–36" (15–91 cm)

Flower: star-shaped yellow flower, 1½–2" (4–5 cm) wide, has 10 pointed orange-streaked petals (broadest at their middles) around many frilly yellow flower parts and is backed by 5 pointed green sepals

Leaf: lance-shaped basal leaves, 1–4" (2.5–10 cm) long, have tiny hook-shaped hairs, lobed or toothed edges, and are easily detached; upper leaves clasp the stem

Fruit: hairy, cylindrical, greenish-tan capsule, ⅔" (1.6 cm) long, cup-shaped at top, tapered base, wick-like center, and twisted persistent sepals on edges

Bloom: summer, fall

Cycle/Origin: perennial, biennial; native

Habitat: dry, gravelly limestone soils; prairies, pastures, hills

Range: western half of Texas

Notes: The flowers open in late afternoon or early evening. One of more than 12 species in the Mentzelia genus in Texas, most of which have unusually intricate flowers. The seedpods are as complex as the flowers. Each seedpod resembles a candle with a wick in the center, but the top rim is ringed with persistent spider-like sepals. Often called Prairie Stickleaf for its habitat and the clinging property of its barbed leaves, which stick to fur and to pant legs. Ranges into southeastern Colorado, Oklahoma, and eastern New Mexico.

FLOWER TYPE
Regular

LEAF TYPE
Simple

LEAF TYPE
Simple Lobed

LEAF ATTACHMENT
Alternate

FRUIT
Pod

373

Cowpen Daisy
Verbesina encelioides

Family: Aster (Asteraceae)

Height: 4–20" (10–50 cm)

Flower: yellow flower head, 1½–2" (4–5 cm) wide, has layers of 12–15 (or many more) overlapping rectangular petals (ray flowers) with 3-lobed tips, surrounding a wide orange center (disk flowers); backed by many pointed, grayish-green bracts

Leaf: broadly triangular leaves, ½–6" (3–15 cm) long, are grayish green and have irregular-toothed margins; lower leaves mostly alternate, upper leaves opposite; opposite pairs of smaller, leaf-like appendages (stipules) at base of each leafstalk

Bloom: summer, fall

Cycle/Origin: annual; native

Habitat: prairies, roadsides, along streams

Range: throughout, but especially along the Rio Grande

Notes: A common annual abundant along roads and in sandy floodplains near washes and streams. Avoided by livestock, this is one of the few plants that remains uneaten where cattle have been confined, thus the common name. Eye-catching, bright-yellow blooms top this upright plant. Also called Golden Crownbeard for the seed-like fruit topped with gray-brown hairs. Ants, birds, and rodents eat the fruit. American Indians used infusions of plant parts to treat skin diseases and spider bites, and they drank it as a tea to treat stomach disorders.

FLOWER TYPE
Composite

LEAF TYPE
Simple

LEAF ATTACHMENT
Alternate

LEAF ATTACHMENT
Opposite

Stiff Greenthread

Thelesperma filifolium

Family: Aster (Asteraceae)

Height: 12–30" (30–76 cm)

Flower: golden-yellow flower head, 1½–2" (4–5 cm) wide, has 8 petals (ray flowers) with 3–lobed tips around a yellow or reddish-brown center (disk flowers); single blooms atop slender, leafless flower stalks

Leaf: frilly leaves, 2–4" (5–10 cm) long, are deeply divided 1–3 times into narrow thread-like lobes; oppositely attached to thin branching stem

Bloom: any season, except in the coldest winter weather

Cycle/Origin: annual, perennial; native

Habitat: shallow soils often with limestone, disturbed areas, along roads, abandoned fields, prairies, rocky slopes, dunes

Range: throughout

Notes: A short-lived perennial or annual herb with thread-like foliage and bright-yellow flowers. Found throughout the Great Plains from South Dakota to Texas and in the Southwest. Also called Navajo Tea because the Navajo and Hopi Indians historically brewed the leaves into a tea to treat urinary tract problems. Deer do not usually eat Stiff Greenthread, but it is food for the caterpillars of Dainty Sulphur butterflies. Finches, such as the colorful Painted Bunting, like the seeds.

FLOWER TYPE
Composite

LEAF TYPE
Simple Lobed

LEAF ATTACHMENT
Opposite

Yellow Sweet Clover

Melilotus officinalis

Family: Pea or Bean (Fabaceae)

Height: 3–6' (.9–1.8 m)

Flower: spike cluster, 1½–5" (4–13 cm) long, of yellow flowers; each flower is ¼" (.6 cm) long

Leaf: each leaf is made up of 3 narrow, toothed, lance-shaped leaflets, ½–1" (1–2.5 cm) long; leaves are alternately attached to branching stem

Fruit: egg-shaped green pod, ¼" (.6 cm) long, turns brown at maturity

Bloom: late spring, summer, sometimes fall

Cycle/Origin: annual, biennial; nonnative

Habitat: agricultural areas, roadsides, along railroads, open fields, waste areas, sun

Range: northern half of Texas

Notes: This nonnative plant was introduced from Europe via Eurasia. Once grown as a hay crop, it has escaped cultivation and now grows throughout Texas along roads and fields. When crushed, the leaves and flowers smell like vanilla. Appropriately in the genus Melilotus, which is Greek for "honey," as bees produce honey from the nectar of this plant. The leaves are eaten by White-tailed and Mule Deer. The rodenticide warfarin was developed from the chemical dicoumarin, which is found in sweet clover.

CLUSTER TYPE	FLOWER TYPE	LEAF TYPE	LEAF ATTACHMENT	LEAF ATTACHMENT	FRUIT
Spike	**Irregular**	**Compound**	**Alternate**	**Basal**	**Pod**

Red Dome Blanketflower
Gaillardia pinnatifida

Family: Aster (Asteraceae)

Height: 6–16" (15–40 cm)

Flower: yellow flower head, 2" (5 cm) wide, has 5–14 short or long petals (ray flowers) with 3–lobed tips around a fuzzy, domed, dark-red center (disk flowers)

Leaf: finely haired basal leaves, 1–2½" (2.5–6 cm) long, are grayish green and lance-shaped to thin; some leaves on each plant have rounded lobes

Bloom: spring, summer, fall

Cycle/Origin: perennial; native

Habitat: plains, mesas, clearings among Ponderosa Pines

Range: western and northwestern Texas

Notes: Red Dome Blanketflower ranges west to southeastern Nevada and north to western Oklahoma. Often found along roads. Frequently included in western wildflower seed mixtures, as it grows readily from seed. The basal clump of leaves sends up long, slim flower stalks, so the blooms bounce and sway in the wind. There are two varieties of this wildflower found in Texas. This variety has more undivided and narrower leaves than the wider, many-lobed leaves of the second type. The genus Gaillardia was named after M. Gaillard de Charentonneau, a French magistrate who supported the studies of botanists in the 18th century.

FLOWER TYPE
Composite

LEAF TYPE
Simple

LEAF TYPE
Simple Lobed

LEAF ATTACHMENT
Alternate

LEAF ATTACHMENT
Basal

Chocolate Flower

Berlandiera lyrata

Family: Aster (Asteraceae)

Height: 5–18" (13–45 cm)

Flower: daisy-like yellow flower head, 2" (5 cm) wide, has 8 yellow petals (ray flowers) with red stripes below and with notched tips; button-like maroon and orange center; each bloom supported by layers of cup-shaped green sepals (calyx)

Leaf: velvety, pale-green leaves, 2–5½" (5–14 cm) long, are oblong with wider tips, irregularly lobed, and on leafstalks

Bloom: spring, summer, fall

Cycle/Origin: perennial; native

Habitat: rocky limestone soils, roadsides, grasslands with oak and juniper trees, open woods, prairies

Range: western Texas

Notes: This wildflower blooms at night, releases a strong chocolate scent in the morning and drops its petals with the increasing heat of the day. The fragrance comes from the flower parts (stamens), which actually taste like unsweetened chocolate. The calyx (see inset) flattens and makes a convenient holder on which the large brown seeds will ripen. Collected and dried before the seeds drop, these calyxes make beautiful additions to dried flower arrangements. Species name lyrata is for the lyre-shaped leaves, referring to the musical instrument played by the ancient Greeks.

FLOWER TYPE
Composite

LEAF TYPE
Simple Lobed

LEAF ATTACHMENT
Alternate

LEAF ATTACHMENT
Basal

Carolina False Dandelion

Pyrrhopappus carolinianus

Family: Aster (Asteraceae)

Height: 6–20" (15–50 cm)

Flower: dandelion-like, bright-yellow flower head, 2" (5 cm) wide, is made up of narrow oblong petals (ray flowers) with fringed tips; pointed, vase-shaped green bracts clasp the flower head that tops a long slender stalk; 1 to several flower heads per plant

Leaf: dandelion-like basal leaves, 3–10" (7.5–25 cm) long, edges with small irregular teeth or deeply lobed with a few long, irregular, narrow projections; basal leaves form a dense rosette; a few stem leaves are attached to the smooth or slightly hairy stem

Bloom: spring, summer

Cycle/Origin: annual, biennial; native

Habitat: dry soils, open woods, disturbed areas, lawns, sun

Range: eastern third of Texas

Notes: Commonly called a false dandelion for the similarity of this annual to Common Dandelion (pg. 363), but it is taller and has fewer stem leaves than that common lawn weed. Unlike Common Dandelion, the stems exude a milky sap when broken or cut. Early-rising sweat bees, the main pollinators of this early morning bloom, tear open the flower parts (anthers) and remove the pollen before other bees become active.

FLOWER TYPE
Composite

LEAF TYPE
Simple

LEAF TYPE
Simple Lobed

LEAF ATTACHMENT
Alternate

LEAF ATTACHMENT
Basal

385

Desert Marigold
Baileya multiradiata

Family: Aster (Asteraceae)

Height: 8–36" (20–91 cm)

Flower: daisy-like, lemon-yellow flower head, 2" (5 cm) wide, of multiple layers of 34–55 overlapping petals with tooth-like edges, surrounding as many as 100 tiny disk flowers; flower head on long flower stalk

Leaf: rosette of oval, grayish-green basal leaves, 1¼–4" (3–10 cm) long, are fuzzy with edges smooth or lobed and resemble the barbs of a feather; stem leaves are much fewer and smaller in the summer

Bloom: spring, summer, fall; after rainfall

Cycle/Origin: annual, perennial, biennial; native

Habitat: deserts, vacant lots, slopes, along roads, mesas

Range: far western Texas, west of the Pecos River

Notes: This Southwestern native is found in only a few counties in far western Texas, but it is one of most common and longest-blooming wildflowers of that region. Desert Marigolds mixed in with bluebonnets often cover hillsides with a yellow-and-blue haze in spring. Poisonous to sheep and goats, it contains chemicals proven to have anticancer properties. Easily grown from seed, but intolerant of temperatures below 32°F (0°C).

FLOWER TYPE
Composite

LEAF TYPE
Simple Lobed

LEAF ATTACHMENT
Alternate

LEAF ATTACHMENT
Basal

Plains Wallflower
Erysimum asperum

Family: Mustard (Brassicaceae)

Height: 6–14" (15–36 cm)

Flower: round or cylindrical, yellow-to-orange-to-reddish-orange cluster, 2–4" (5–10 cm) wide, of many small flowers; each flower, ¾" (2 cm) wide, has 4 oval petals and protruding green flower parts; clusters bloom from the bottom up

Leaf: long, narrow leaves, 1–5" (2.5–13 cm) long, have pointed tips and are dense along and alternately attached to a rough, hairy stem

Fruit: thin, fleshy green pod, turning brown, 3" (7.5 cm) long, has 4 sides and grows at right angles to stem

Bloom: early spring, summer

Cycle/Origin: perennial, biennial; native

Habitat: prairies, woodlands, cliffs, slopes, canyons

Range: central and western Texas

Notes: "Wallflower" comes from a close relative from Eurasia that is often found growing on stone walls. One of the largest and most conspicuous mustards. Mustard family members have been developed into cultivated food plants such as radish, turnip, and cauliflower. Less usefully, other mustards have become invasive weeds in agricultural fields. Hybridizes with other wallflower species. Range of Western Wallflower (*E. capitatum;* not shown) overlaps with Plains in Texas, but Western has upright seedpods.

CLUSTER TYPE	FLOWER TYPE	LEAF TYPE	LEAF ATTACHMENT	LEAF ATTACHMENT	FRUIT
Round	**Regular**	**Simple**	**Alternate**	**Basal**	**Pod**

Bitterweed

Hymenoxys odorata

Family: Aster (Asteraceae)

Height: 6–24" (15–61 cm)

Flower: daisy-like yellow flower head, 2½" (6 cm) wide, composed of 8–13 petals (ray flowers) with 3-lobed tips around a raised button-like yellow center (disk flowers); 15–350 blossoms per plant

Leaf: thread-like, grayish-green leaves, ½–2" (1–5 cm) long, dotted with glands, irregularly divided into narrow lobes and alternately attached to stem that branches throughout its length

Bloom: spring, summer

Cycle/Origin: annual; native

Habitat: ditches, roadsides, mesquite woodlands, overgrazed rangelands, along streams and stream bottoms

Range: western half of Texas

Notes: An upright branching annual, Bitterweed is found throughout the Southwest. The thread-like, resin-dotted leaves decrease the amount of moisture lost through evaporation, making this aster well adapted to arid conditions. A poisonous (potentially lethal) weed usually avoided by livestock due to its bitter taste, but still a problem for ranchers in western Texas, since sheep will eat it when other forage is scarce. Causes gastric irritation, liver and kidney failure.

FLOWER TYPE
Composite

LEAF TYPE
Simple

LEAF TYPE
Simple Lobed

LEAF ATTACHMENT
Alternate

Black-eyed Susan
Rudbeckia hirta

Family: Aster (Asteraceae)

Height: 12–36" (30–91 cm)

Flower: daisy-like yellow flower head, 2–3" (5–7.5 cm) wide, with 10–20 petals (ray flowers) around a raised button-like brown center (disk flowers); 1 to numerous large flower heads per plant

Leaf: lance-shaped or elliptical leaves, 2–7" (5–18 cm) long, are slender, very hairy, toothless, and alternately attached; winged leafstalk clasps a hairy stem

Bloom: spring, summer, sometimes fall

Cycle/Origin: annual, perennial, biennial; native

Habitat: dry, sandy soils; open woods, prairies, fields

Range: eastern half of Texas

Notes: Also called Brown-eyed Susan, but just who "Susan" was remains unknown. Look for three prominent veins on each leaf and a characteristic winged leafstalk clasping each upright, straight stem. Species name hirta is Latin for "hairy" or "rough" and refers to the plant's hairy stems and leaves. Originally a native prairie plant, it has been widely cultivated and is now found in just about any habitat. Seeds are an abundant food source for goldfinches, and the flowers attract butterflies. A host plant for the black-with-orange-striped caterpillars of the Silvery Checkerspot butterfly. The caterpillars camouflage themselves with bits of the flower secured by silk while feeding on the brown centers of Black-eyed Susan.

FLOWER TYPE **Composite**   LEAF TYPE **Simple**   LEAF ATTACHMENT **Alternate**   LEAF ATTACHMENT **Clasping**

Maximilian Sunflower
Helianthus maximiliani

Family: Aster (Asteraceae)

Height: 3–10' (.9–3 m)

Flower: yellow flower heads, 2–3" (5–7.5 cm) wide, each made of 20–40 petals (ray flowers) surrounding a yellow center (disk flowers); blooms spiral around the upper stem

Leaf: narrow, lance-shaped, grayish-green leaves, 4–12" (10–30 cm) long, are rough to the touch and folded lengthwise; the leaves and reddish-green stem are covered with white hairs

Bloom: late summer, fall

Cycle/Origin: perennial; native

Habitat: prairies, along roads and streams, rocky ledges, disturbed areas

Range: throughout Texas, except the far western and far eastern edges of the state

Notes: This tall plant with its big flowers usually grows in large colonies, producing chemicals that retard the growth of other plants. American Indians used the seeds, fibers, and petals for sources of food, oil, thread, and dye. Sioux Indians also ate the thick root, which tastes similar to that of Jerusalem Artichoke (*H. tuberosus;* not shown). Its seeds are consumed by sparrows, finches, and quail. Pioneers planted this sunflower near their houses to repel mosquitoes and sprinkled the petals in bath water to relieve arthritis.

FLOWER TYPE	LEAF TYPE	LEAF ATTACHMENT
Composite	**Simple**	**Alternate**

Ground Plum Milkvetch
Astragalus crassicarpus

Family: Pea or Bean (Fabaceae)

Height: 6–20" (15–50 cm)

Flower: cream-colored or purple flowers in short spike clusters, 2–3" (5–7.5 cm) long; each pea-like bloom, 1" (2.5 cm) long, has an upper petal (standard) and lower petals (keel) that are sometimes pink-tipped

Leaf: feather-like, grayish-green leaves, 2–5" (5–13 cm) long, are divided into 7–16 pairs of hairy, narrow, pointed leaflets

Fruit: round fleshy pod, ½–1" (1–2.5 cm) wide, turning greenish red when mature

Bloom: spring, summer

Cycle/Origin: perennial; native

Habitat: prairies, along roads, thickets, canyons, hillsides, edges of woods

Range: northern two-thirds of Texas

Notes: This member of the Pea or Bean family has sprawling stems with silky-haired, grayish-green foliage and dangling flower spikes of pea-like blossoms. The succulent pods are said to be edible, tasting something like snow peas, and were used like a vegetable by Plains Indians. The dried root was made into a powder and applied to wounds to stop bleeding. Also called Buffalo Plum or Buffalo Bean.

CLUSTER TYPE
Spike

FLOWER TYPE
Irregular

LEAF TYPE
Compound

LEAF ATTACHMENT
Alternate

FRUIT
Pod

fruit

Texas Prickly Pear
Opuntia engelmannii

Family: Cactus (Cactaceae)

Height: 3–10' (.9–3 m); shrub

Flower: cup-shaped yellow (can be red, pink, or orange) flowers, 2–5" (5–13 cm) wide, each with many overlapping petals around a wide yellow-and-green center; blooms grow upright from top edges of thin, flat cactus pads

Leaf: pads have widely spread clusters of 1–6 pale yellow-to-dark-yellow spines, ½–1¼" (1–3 cm) long; can have 1 longest spine, up to 4½" (11 cm) long, in each cluster; stiff yellow bristles encircle each cluster

Fruit: barrel-shaped, dark-red pod, 1¼–3½" (3–9 cm) long, smooth, mostly spineless skin; contains red pulp

Bloom: spring

Cycle/Origin: perennial; native

Habitat: deserts, prairies, open woods, flats, ridges

Range: southern half of Texas

Notes: This short-trunked cactus has large, oval green pads forming a sprawling shrub as wide as 20 feet (6.1 m). Although found in neighboring states, the *lindheimeri* variety is abundant and most common in Texas. Flowers are usually lemon yellow, but flower color can vary, especially on plants near the coast. Also called Candy Apple for the edible, dark-red fruit. Pack rats use the spiny pads to build their nests, forming a protective barrier against predators.

FLOWER TYPE   LEAF TYPE   FRUIT
Regular   **Spines**   **Pod**

Smallflower Fumewort
Corydalis micrantha

Family: Fumitory (Fumariaceae)

Height: 8–16" (20–40 cm)

Flower: yellow spike cluster, 3" (7.5 cm) long, of 10–16 oddly shaped flowers with long spurs that contain nectar; each bloom, ½–1" (1–2.5 cm) long, on a flower stalk just above a small, leaf-like green bract

Leaf: silvery-green basal leaves, 3–6" (7.5–15 cm) long, are compound, on long stalks and divided into oblong leaflets with lobes; upper leaves on shorter stalks alternate on square, reddish-green stems

Fruit: upright, slender, bean-like capsule, 1" (2.5 cm) long, green with small, shiny black seeds when mature

Bloom: late spring, summer

Cycle/Origin: annual; native

Habitat: dry, sandy, or rocky soils; open woods, savannahs

Range: eastern and southern Texas

Notes: A winter annual that grows as a basal rosette of leaves and sends up a flower stalk in late spring. Species name micrantha is for the small seeds that distinguish it from all other yellow-flowered species in the Corydalis genus. These black seeds each have a small, fleshy white appendage that ants like to eat. The ants store the seeds underground for later consumption, thus protecting the seeds from being eaten by rodents. American Indians placed the root on hot coals and inhaled the smoke to clear the sinuses.

CLUSTER TYPE
Spike

FLOWER TYPE
Irregular

LEAF TYPE
Compound

LEAF ATTACHMENT
Alternate

FRUIT
Pod

Common Sunflower
Helianthus annuus

Family: Aster (Asteraceae)

Height: 3–10' (.9–3 m)

Flower: sunny yellow flower head, 3–6" (7.5–15 cm) wide, with 15–20 yellow petals surrounding a large, dark-brown or purple center; 2–20 flowers per plant

Leaf: broadly triangular or heart-shaped leaves, 3–12" (7.5–30 cm) long, stiff hairs, coarsely and irregularly toothed; leaves alternate along a very coarse stem

Bloom: year-round

Cycle/Origin: annual; native

Habitat: fields, along roads, disturbed ground, prairies, stream banks

Range: throughout

Notes: A smaller, wild version of Giant Sunflower, which is the large cultivated plant often grown in gardens and fields and from which seeds are harvested. Unlike the giant variety, Common Sunflower usually branches several times, but it is similar in that it produces many nutritious seeds. Used for food by many peoples historically, the seeds can be ground or pressed to make flour, oil, dyes—even medicine. Often seen growing along highways, where the seeds of maturing plants are dispersed along the road by wind created from passing vehicles. Sunflowers do not follow the sun, as is widely believed. Flower heads face the morning sun once the plant matures and begins to bloom, thus most flowers face east.

FLOWER TYPE   LEAF TYPE   LEAF ATTACHMENT
Composite   **Simple**   **Alternate**

Tall Goldenrod
Solidago altissima

Family: Aster (Asteraceae)

Height: 3–7' (.9–2.1 m)

Flower: mass of large, arching to stiffly upright spike clusters; each spike, 3–9" (7.5–23 cm) long, is made up of tiny yellow flower heads loosely clustered along upper side of stalk

Leaf: narrow, lance-shaped leaves, 1¼–6" (3–15 cm) long, stalkless with a hairy, rough upper surface and shallow, sharp teeth; fewer leaves toward stem base; stem branches near top

Bloom: late summer, fall

Cycle/Origin: perennial; native

Habitat: moist soils, disturbed areas, fields, along streams and reservoirs

Range: throughout, but especially the eastern half of Texas

Notes: One of the latest-blossoming flowers, blooming through fall. This common plant is often seen along roads in patches as wide as 8–30 feet (2.4–9.1 m), excluding other plants from the site. Also called Late Goldenrod, Common Goldenrod, or Field Goldenrod. The 25 species of goldenrod in Texas are hard to positively identify from one another. While most fall-blooming yellow flowers are goldenrods (often blamed for hay fever), autumn allergies are caused mainly by Ragweed (*Ambrosia artemisiifolia;* not shown). Only 1–2% of fall airborne pollen is from goldenrod.

CLUSTER TYPE
Spike

FLOWER TYPE
Composite

LEAF TYPE
Simple

LEAF ATTACHMENT
Alternate

LEAF ATTACHMENT
Basal

fruit

Buffalo Gourd
Cucurbita foetidissima

Family: Gourd (Cucurbitaceae)

Height: 5–20' (1.5–6.1 m); vine

Flower: broad, trumpet-shaped, yellow or orange flowers, 3½–5" (9–13 cm) long, each with petals that flare widely into 5 pointed wrinkled lobes

Leaf: large, heart-shaped leaves, 6–12" (15–30 cm) long, with finely toothed edges, are grayish green above and white below, roughly textured and foul smelling

Fruit: gourd-like, resembling a little round watermelon, 3" (7.5 cm) wide, smooth with green-and-white-stripes, turning all yellow when ripe; pumpkin-like seeds

Bloom: spring, summer, fall

Cycle/Origin: perennial; native

Habitat: dry, sandy soils; disturbed areas, along railroads and streams, roadsides, on fences

Range: central and western Texas, ranging over half of the state

Notes: Also called Coyote Melon and closely related to garden pumpkins. American Indians have used this plant for 9,000 years, extracting oil for cooking from the edible seeds or roasting and salting them to eat. The dried fruit was also picked to make gourd rattles used during ceremonies. The crushed leaves are an effective insecticide, and the fetid-smelling chemicals they contain (thus the species name foetidissima) are being studied for modern uses.

FLOWER TYPE
Tube

LEAF TYPE
Simple

LEAF ATTACHMENT
Alternate

FRUIT
Pod

fruit

American Lotus
Nelumbo lutea

Family: Lotus (Nelumbonaceae)

Height: aquatic

Flower: cup-shaped, pale-yellow flower, 6–10" (15–25 cm) wide, with many large petals surrounding a large yellow center; flowers atop flower stalks that rise up to 12" (30 cm) above the surface of water

Leaf: very large, round leaves, 12–24" (30–61 cm) wide, on leafstalks rising up to 12" (30 cm) above the surface of water; the toothless edges are often upturned to form a shallow bowl

Fruit: round, pod-like green container, turning brown; numerous acorn-like seeds are released through many Swiss cheese-like openings at the top

Bloom: summer, fall

Cycle/Origin: perennial; native

Habitat: small lakes, channels, ponds, slow-moving streams

Range: eastern half of Texas

Notes: The large, round leaves and flowers of this plant (perhaps the largest wildflower in Texas) stand well above the water on stalks, waving in the wind and distinguishing it from those of water lilies, which float on the water. Flowers open only on sunny days. The large seedpods are often used in dried floral arrangements. Its roots are eaten by wildlife. American Indians used the roots and seeds for food, and they also used the seeds for counters and dice in games.

FLOWER TYPE **Regular**   LEAF TYPE **Simple**   LEAF ATTACHMENT **Basal**   FRUIT **Pod**

Texas Ragwort
Senecio ampullaceus

Family: Aster (Asteraceae)

Height: 12–36" (30–91 cm); shrub

Flower: flat-topped yellow clusters, 6–12" (15–30 cm) wide, of 10–30 daisy-like flower heads; each blossom 1" (2.5 cm) wide, has 8 separated, narrow yellow petals (ray flowers) surrounding an orangish-yellow center of disk flowers

Leaf: lance-shaped, grayish-green leaves, 1½–6" (4–15 cm) long, are woolly with long, matted white hairs, have smooth or coarse-toothed edges and broad-winged leafstalks; leaves alternately clasp the stiff stem; upper leaves are smaller

Bloom: early spring, early summer

Cycle/Origin: annual; native

Habitat: disturbed soils, overgrazed rangelands, newly cleared forests, along sandy washes

Range: eastern, southern, coastal, and central Texas

Notes: A many-stemmed, multi-branched, grayish-green shrub with flat clusters of bright-yellow flowers atop long flower stalks that extend well above the leaves. Toxic if eaten and usually avoided by livestock; hungry animals that do consume the young plants show signs of liver damage. Abundant in disturbed soils, helping other plants to become established by stabilizing the soil. Can overtake rangeland that has been overgrazed, forming solid carpets of yellow.

CLUSTER TYPE	FLOWER TYPE	LEAF TYPE	LEAF ATTACHMENT	LEAF ATTACHMENT
Flat	**Composite**	**Simple**	**Alternate**	**Clasping**

fruit

Longbract Wild Indigo
Baptisia bracteata

Family: Pea or Bean (Fabaceae)

Height: 18–30" (45–76 cm); shrub

Flower: drooping spike cluster, 8–12" (20–30 cm) long, of large, pea-like, creamy-yellow flowers; each flower, 1½" (4 cm) long; 1 to a few spikes per plant

Leaf: leathery, compound leaves made up of 3 leaflets; each oval leaflet, 1–3" (2.5–7.5 cm) long, widest near the tip and hairy; leaves on short stalks; hairy stem

Fruit: swollen green pod, ¾" (2 cm) long, with a pointed "beak," turns charcoal black with age

Bloom: very early to late spring

Cycle/Origin: perennial; native

Habitat: limestone soils, prairies, pastures, woodland openings, along roads

Range: eastern half of Texas

Notes: The species name bracteata refers to the large, leaf-like bract that grows below each flower. Forms an attractive, low, mounded, blue-green bush with long yellow flower spikes drooping below the foliage and sprawling on the ground. Often cultivated, its charcoal-black seedpods are used in floral arrangements. Pollinated mainly in early spring by queen bumblebees after they emerge from hibernation. The leaves are eaten by the caterpillars of Southern Dogface and Orange Sulphur butterflies but are poisonous to livestock.

CLUSTER TYPE	FLOWER TYPE	LEAF TYPE	LEAF ATTACHMENT	FRUIT
Spike	**Irregular**	**Compound**	**Alternate**	**Pod**

fruit

Maryland Senna

Senna marilandica

Family: Pea or Bean (Fabaceae)

Height: 3–8' (.9–2.4 m)

Flower: upright spike clusters, 8–12" (20–30 cm) long, of yellow flowers; each blossom, ¾" (2 cm) wide, looks regular but is actually irregular, with unequal-size petals around dark reddish-brown flower parts

Leaf: compound leaves are feathery, on long stalks and divided into 4–8 pairs of oblong leaflets, 1–2" (2.5–5 cm) long, each with a rounded end; green gland near base of each leafstalk

Fruit: drooping, hairy green pod, 3" (7.5 cm) long, turns black and curving, remaining on stem in winter

Bloom: summer

Cycle/Origin: perennial; native

Habitat: moist soils, woodland edges, open pastures

Range: eastern Texas

Notes: The feathery leaves of Maryland Senna provide an attractive accent in a restored prairie patch or native wildflower meadow. The dried plant with its black seedpods is ornamental in winter. Pollinated mainly by bumblebees, which eat the pollen. A dome-shaped gland near the base of each leafstalk secretes nectar to attract ants and ladybird beetles, which drink the nectar and are thought to protect the plant from other insects that might eat the foliage. The plant is used as an ingredient in strong laxatives.

CLUSTER TYPE	FLOWER TYPE	LEAF TYPE	LEAF ATTACHMENT	FRUIT
Spike	**Irregular**	**Compound**	**Alternate**	**Pod**

Common Mullein
Verbascum thapsus

Family: Snapdragon (Scrophulariaceae)

Height: 2–6' (.6–1.8 m)

Flower: club-like spike cluster, 12–24" (30–61 cm) long, of many small yellow flowers packed along the stalk, opening only a few at a time, from the top down; each flower, ¾–1" (2–2.5 cm) wide, has 5 petals

Leaf: large basal leaves, 12–15" (30–38 cm) long, are velvety with a thick covering of stiff hairs; stalkless upper leaves clasp main stem at alternate intervals; leaves are progressively smaller toward top of stalk

Bloom: spring, summer, fall

Cycle/Origin: biennial; nonnative

Habitat: any habitat, but usually in disturbed sites

Range: throughout Texas, especially in the eastern half of the state

Notes: A European import known for its very soft, flannel-like leaves, hence its other common name, Flannel Plant. This biennial takes two years to mature. The first year it grows as a low rosette of large, soft leaves; in the second, a tall flower stalk sprouts. Its dried stems stand well into winter. It is said the Romans dipped its dried flower stalks in animal tallow to use as torches. Victorian women rubbed the leaves on their cheeks, slightly irritating their skin, to add a dash of blush. Early settlers and American Indians placed the soft, woolly leaves in footwear for warmth and comfort.

USTER TYPE
Spike

FLOWER TYPE
Regular

LEAF TYPE
Simple

LEAF ATTACHMENT
Alternate

LEAF ATTACHMENT
Clasping

LEAF ATTACHMENT
Basal

GLOSSARY

Alternate: A type of leaf attachment in which the leaves are singly and alternately attached along a stem, not paired or in whorls.

Annual: A plant that germinates, flowers, and sets seed during a single growing season and returns the following year from seed only.

Anther: A portion of the male flower part that contains the pollen. See *stamen*.

Axis: A point on the main stem from which lateral branches arise.

Basal: The leaves at the base of a plant near the ground, usually grouped in a round rosette.

Bell flower: A single, downward-hanging flower that has petals fused together, forming a bell-like shape. See *tube flower*.

Berry: A fleshy fruit that contains one or many seeds.

Biennial: A plant that lives for two years, blooming in the second year.

Bract: A leaf-like structure usually found at the base of a flower, often appearing as a petal.

Bulb: A short, round, underground shoot that is used as a food storage system, common in the Lily family.

Calyx: A collective group of all of the sepals of a flower.

Capsule: A pod-like fruiting structure that contains many seeds and has more than one chamber. See *pod*.

Cauline: The leaves that attach to the stem distinctly above the ground, as opposed to basal leaves, which attach near the ground.

Clasping: A type of leaf attachment in which the leaf base partly surrounds the main stem of the plant at the point of attachment; grasping the stem without a leafstalk.

Cluster: A group or collection of flowers or leaves.

Composite flower: A collection of tiny or small flowers that appears as one large flower, usually made up of ray and disk flowers, common in the Aster family.

Compound leaf: A single leaf composed of a central stalk and two or more leaflets.

Corolla: All of the petals of a flower that fuse together to form a tube.

Creosote bush: A yellow-flowered evergreen bush with a resinous odor, most strongly fragrant after rainfall, abundant in Southwest deserts.

Disk flower: One of many tiny, tubular flowers in the central part (disk) of a composite flower, common in the Aster family.

Ephemeral: Lasting for only a short time each spring.

Flat cluster: A group of flowers that forms a flat-topped structure, which allows flying insects to easily land and complete pollination.

Floret: One of many smaller flowers that make up a flower head.

Gland: A tiny structure that usually secretes oil or nectar, sometimes found on leaves, stems, stalks, and flowers, as in Curlycup Gumweed.

Globular: Having a spherical or globe-like shape.

Irregular flower: A flower that does not have the typical round shape, usually made up of five or more petals that are fused together in an irregular shape, common in the Pea or Bean family.

Keel: The two lower petals, often fused together, of a flower in the Pea or Bean family.

Leaflet: One of two or more leaf-like parts of a compound leaf.

Lip: The projection of a flower petal or the "odd" petal, such as the large inflated petal common in the Snapdragon family; sometimes, the lobes of a petal. See *lobe*.

Lobe: A large rounded projection of a petal or leaf, larger than the tooth of a leaf.

Lobed leaf: A simple leaf with at least one indentation (sinus) along an edge that does not reach the center or base of the leaf, as in Common Dandelion.

Margin: The edge of a leaf.

Mesa: An elevated, flat expanse of land (plateau), with one or more steep sides or cliffs; Spanish for "tableland."

Node: The place or point of origin on a stem where leaves attach or have been attached.

Nutlet: A small or diminutive nut or seed.

Opposite: A type of leaf attachment in which pairs of leaves are situated directly across from each other on a stem.

Palmate leaf: A type of compound leaf in which three or more leaflets arise from a common central point at the end of a leafstalk, as in Texas Bluebonnet.

Parasitic: A plant or fungus that derives its food or water chiefly from another plant, to the detriment of the host plant. See *semiparasitic*.

Perennial: A plant that lives from several to many seasons, returning each year from its roots.

Perfoliate: A type of leaf attachment in which the bases of at least two leaves connect around the main stem so that the stem appears to pass through one stalkless leaf.

Petal: A basic flower part that is usually brightly colored, serving to attract pollinating insects.

Photosynthesis: In green plants, the conversion of water and carbon dioxide into carbohydrates (food) from the energy in sunlight.

Pistil: The female part of a flower made up of an ovary, style, and stigma, often in the center of the flower.

Pod: A dry fruiting structure that contains many seeds, often with a single chamber. See *capsule*.

Pollination: The transfer of pollen from the male anther to the female stigma, usually resulting in the production of seeds.

Ray flower: One of many individual outer flowers of a composite flower, common in the Aster family.

Recurved: Curved backward or downward, as in bracts or sepals.

Regular flower: A flower with 3–20 typical petals that are arranged in a circle.

Rhizome: A creeping, (usually) horizontal, underground stem.

Rosette: A cluster of leaves arranged in a circle, often at the base of the plant, as in Common Mullein.

Round cluster: A group of many flowers that forms a round structure, giving the appearance of one large flower.

Seed head: A group or cluster of seeds

Semiparasitic: A type of plant or fungus that derives a portion, but not all, of its food or water from another plant, possibly to the detriment of the host plant. See *parasitic*.

Sepal: A member of the outermost set of petals of a flower, typically green and leaf-like, but often colored and resembling a petal.

Simple leaf: A single leaf with an undivided or unlobed edge.

Spike cluster: A group of many flowers on a single, spike-like stem, giving the appearance of one large flower.

Spine: A modified leaf; a stiff, usually short, sharply pointed outgrowth. See *thorn*.

Spur: A hollow, tube-like appendage of a flower, usually where nectar is located, as in Red Columbine.

Stamen: The male parts of a flower, each consisting of a filament and an anther. See *anther*.

Standard: The uppermost petal of a flower in the Pea or Bean family.

Stem leaf: Any leaf that grows along the stem of a plant, as opposed to a leaf at the base of a plant. See *cauline* and *basal*.

Stigma: The female part of the flower that receives the pollen.

Stipule: A basal appendage (usually in pairs) of a leaf that is not attached to the leaf blade, as in Everlasting Pea.

Taproot: The primary, vertically descending root of a plant.

Tendril: A twining, string-like structure of a vine that clings to plants or other objects for support.

Terminal: Growing at the end of a leaf, stem, or stalk.

Thorn: A modified part of a stem; a stiff, usually long and sharply pointed outgrowth. See *spine*.

Throat: The opening or orifice of a tubular flower (corolla or calyx).

Toothed: Having a jagged or serrated edge of a leaf, resembling teeth of a saw.

Tube flower: A flower with fused petals forming a tube and usually turned upward. See *bell flower*.

Umbel: A domed to relatively flat-topped flower cluster that resembles the overall shape of an open umbrella, common in the Carrot family.

Wash: A usually dry and sandy streambed in the Southwest over which water flows during or after heavy rains.

Whorl: A type of attachment in which a circle or ring of three or more similar leaves, stems, or flowers originates from a common point.

Wing: A flat extension at the base of a leaf or edge of a leafstalk, sometimes extending down the stem of the plant; one of the side petals of a flower, common in the Pea or Bean family.

Woody: Having the appearance or texture resembling wood, as in stems, bark, or taproots.

CHECKLIST/INDEX BY SPECIES

Use the boxes to check the flowers you've seen.

☐ Alfalfa 189

☐ Arrowhead, Broadleaf 301

☐ Aster, Meadow 185

☐ Aster, Southern Annual . . . 255

☐ Aster, Spiny 251

☐ Baby Blue Eyes, Largeflower 21

☐ Basketflower, American . . . 219

☐ Beardtongue, Cobaea 147

☐ Beardtongue, Nodding. . . . 145

☐ Beardtongue, Scarlet. 239

☐ Bee Balm, Lemon. 117

☐ Bee Balm, Spotted 105

☐ Beeblossom, Scarlet 137

☐ Bergamot, Wild 191

☐ Betony, Texas 237

☐ Bindweed, Field. 275

☐ Bitterweed. 391

☐ Black-eyed Susan. 393

☐ Bladderpod, Fendler 327

☐ Bladderpod, Gordon 321

☐ Blanketflower, Red Dome . . 381

☐ Blazing Star, Dotted 213

☐ Blazing Star, Reverchon . . . 373

☐ Bluebill 195

☐ Bluebonnet, Sandyland . . . 43

☐ Bluebonnet, Texas 53

☐ Bluebowls. 171

☐ Blue-eyed Grass, Roadside 19

☐ Bluet, Prairie 267

☐ Bluet, Tiny. 77

☐ Briar, Nuttall Sensitive 95

☐ Bristlemallow, Carolina 81

☐ Broomweed, Prairie 319

☐ Buffalo Gourd. 407

☐ Bullnettle, Texas 299

☐ Bush Sunflower, Awnless 351

☐ Buttercup, Large 345

☐ Butterflyweed. 67

☐ Camas, Atlantic 51

☐ Camphorweed 325

☐ Camphorweed, Sweetscent 143

☐ Cardinalflower 243

☐ Catchfly, Cardinal 227

☐ Caterpillars 207

☐ Chocolate Flower 383

☐ Clammyweed, Red Whisker. 289

☐ Clover, Black Prairie 101

☐ Clover, White 263

☐ Clover, Yellow Sweet 379

☐ Columbine, Red. 229

☐ Coneflower, Sanguine Purple 215

☐ Coneflower, Upright Prairie 339

☐ Cornflower, Garden. 27

☐ Crownbeard, White 313

☐ Crow Poison. 253

☐ Cypress, Standing. 69

☐ Daisy, Arkansas Doze. 259

☐ Daisy, Blackfoot. 269

☐ Daisy, Butterfly 359

☐ Daisy, Cowpen. 375

☐ Daisy, Engelmann. 369

☐ Daisy, Plains Yellow 365

☐ Daisy, Texas Sleepy. 367

☐ Dandelion, Carolina False. 385

☐ Dandelion, Common 363

☐ Datura, Sacred 307

☐ Dayflower, Whitemouth 25

☐ Deadnettle, Henbit. 131

☐ Deadnettle, Purple 205

☐ Devil's Bouquet. 231

☐ Dogbane, Spreading 73

☐ Dogweed. 315

☐ Dragonhead, Showy False. 135

☐ Eryngo, Leavenworth 179

☐ Fanpetals, Spreading. 329

☐ Filaree 181

☐ Five Eyes, Greenleaf 323

☐ Flax, Berlandier. 59

☐ Fleabane, Philadelphia . . . 261

☐ Fleabane, Plains 257

☐ Four O'clock, Trailing. 183

☐ Foxglove, Prairie False 99

☐ Frogfruit, Texas 273

☐ Fumewort, Smallflower . . . 401

☐ Fuzzybean, Slickseed. 83

☐ Gentian, Prairie Rose. 97

☐ Gentian, Showy Prairie. . . . 35

☐ Geranium, Carolina. 249

☐ Germander, Canada 153

☐ Gilia, Scarlet. 241

☐ Globemallow, Copper 155

☐ Goldenaster, Hoary False 331

☐ Goldenrod, Tall 405

☐ Greenthread, Stiff. 377

☐ Gumweed, Curlycup 353

☐ Herb of Grace. 247

☐ Indian Blanket 65

☐ Indigo, Longbract Wild 413

☐ Iris, Virginia 41

☐ Ironweed, Baldwin 221

☐ Lady's Tresses, Spring 293

☐ Lantana, Texas 61

☐ Larkspur, Carolina 55

☐ Lily, Evening Rain 295

☐ Lotus, American. 409

☐ Lythrum, Winged 151

☐ Mallow, Wax 225

☐ Marigold, Desert 387

☐ Milkvetch, Ground Plum . . . 397

☐ Milkvetch, Smallflower. . . . 161

☐ Milkweed, Spider 57

☐ Milkwort, White 281

☐ Mistflower, Blue. 47

☐ Mullein, Common. 417

☐ Nama, Bristly 163

☐ Nightshade, Silverleaf 175

☐ Onion, Drummond 157

☐ Paintbrush, Downy 149

☐ Paintbrush, Entireleaf Indian 63

☐ Palafox, Rose 89

☐ Palafox, Sand 113

☐ Pansy, Field 167

☐ Passionflower, Purple 199

☐ Pea, Everlasting. 109

☐ Pea, Partridge 347

☐ Pea, Scarlet 159

☐ Pea, Spurred Butterfly 193

☐ Petunia, Western Wild 217

☐ Phlox, Annual 133

☐ Phlox, Downy 129

☐ Pickerelweed 45

☐ Pink, Mountain 75

☐ Plantain, Woolly 283

☐ Pleatleaf, Prairie 37

☐ Plume, Feather 107

☐ Pokeweed 311

☐ Polkadots 177

☐ Poorjoe 71

☐ Poppy, Bluestem Prickly . . . 297

☐ Poppy, Red Prickly 235

☐ Prairie Nymph. 203

☐ Prickly Pear, Texas 399

☐ Primrose, Showy Evening 127

425

☐ Primrosewillow, Mexican. . . 361

☐ Puccoon, Narrowleaf 371

☐ Puffballs 271

☐ Purslane, Shaggy 79

☐ Ragwort, Texas 411

☐ Rain Lily, Evening 295

☐ Ram's Horn 125

☐ Ratany, Trailing 93

☐ Resinbush 341

☐ Rose, Texas Rock 111

☐ Rosemallow,
Crimsoneyed 303

☐ Rouge Plant 141

☐ Sage, Autumn 103

☐ Sage, Azure Blue 49

☐ Sage, Mealycup 39

☐ Sage, Tropical 233

☐ Sandmat, Whitemargin . . . 245

☐ Selfheal, Common 31

☐ Senna, Maryland 415

☐ Sensitive Briar, Nuttall 95

☐ Skeleton Plant, Texas 119

☐ Skullcap, Drummond 165

☐ Smartweed, Curlytop 87

☐ Snakeroot, White 279

☐ Snakeweed, Broom 317

☐ Snapdragonvine 169

☐ Sneezeweed,
Slenderleaf 337

☐ Snow on the Mountain . . . 285

☐ Sowthistle, Spiny 343

☐ Spiderlily, Spring 309

☐ Spiderwort, Prairie 33

☐ Spring Beauty 85

☐ Standing Cypress 69

☐ Sundrops, Hartweg 355

☐ Sunflower,
Awnless Bush 351

☐ Sunflower, Common 403

☐ Sunflower, Maximilian . . . 395

☐ Tansyaster, Lacy 333

☐ Tansyaster, Tansyleaf 187

☐ Tephrosia, Virginia 123

☐ Thimbleweed, Tenpetal . . . 265

☐ Thistle, Horrid 211

☐ Thistle, Texas 115

☐ Thoroughwort,
Lateflowering 305

☐ Tickseed, Golden 357

☐ Tievine 139

☐ Toadflax, Bastard 277

☐ Toadflax, Texas 209

☐ Twinevine, Fringed 201

☐ Venus's Looking Glass, Clasping 173

☐ Vervain, Dakota Mock 197

☐ Vervain, Texas 223

☐ Violet, Common Blue 23

☐ Wallflower, Plains 389

☐ Waterleaf, Blue 29

☐ Waterlily, White 291

☐ Wine Cup 121

☐ Wood Sorrel, Drummond . . . 91

☐ Yarrow, Common 287

☐ Yellowstar, Texas 335

☐ Zinnia, Plains 349

PHOTO CREDITS

All photos are copyright of their respective photographers.

NOTES

ABOUT THE AUTHORS

Nora Mays Bowers

Nora Mays Bowers is a writer and nature photographer. She earned a Master of Science degree in Ecology from the University of Arizona, writing her thesis and publishing several professional papers on Harris's hawks. Nora has received numerous grants and awards for her hawk research. Nora's photography credits include *Birder's World* magazine, *Ranger Rick*, and *Arizona Wildlife Views*, as well as in many books and calendars. She is a coauthor of *Wildflowers of Arizona Field Guide*, *Cactus of Arizona Field Guide*, *Cactus of the Southwest*, and *Kaufman Focus Guides: Mammals of North America*.

Rick Bowers

Rick Bowers is a tour leader, nature photographer, naturalist, and writer. He has been photographing wildlife and nature for almost 50 years. He received a Bachelor of Science degree in Wildlife Ecology from the University of Arizona. He lived and birded in Europe for six years as an Army "brat." Subsequently, Rick led nature tours for Victor Emanuel Nature Tours for 16 years. Rick led tours throughout the New World from Barrow, Alaska (the northernmost city in North America), to Tierra del Fuego (an island at the southern tip of South America) and Antarctica. He has led tours in the Old World to southern Africa and to the Kamchatka Peninsula of Siberia, as well as to Australia. Rick's photo credits span the gamut, from *National Geographic* and *International Wildlife* magazines to state and local fish and game publications. He is a coauthor of *Wildflowers of Arizona Field Guide*, *Cactus of Arizona Field Guide*, and *Kaufman Focus Guides: Mammals of North America*. He now owns Bowers Birding and Photo Safaris and leads international birding and photo safaris to Borneo, India, and Malaysia, as well as private tours in the US.

Nora and Rick live in Tucson, Arizona. They can be reached through their webpage at www.bowersphoto.com.

Stan Tekiela

Naturalist, wildlife photographer, and writer Stan Tekiela is the originator of the popular state-specific field guide series that includes *Birds of Texas Field Guide*. Stan has authored more than 190 educational books, including field guides, quick guides, nature books, children's books, playing cards, and more, presenting many species of animals and plants.

With a Bachelor of Science degree in Natural History from the University of Minnesota and as an active professional naturalist for more than 30 years, Stan studies and photographs wildlife throughout the United States and Canada. He has received various national and regional awards for his books and photographs. Also a well-known columnist and radio personality, his syndicated column appears in more than 25 newspapers, and his wildlife programs are broadcast on a number of Midwest radio stations. Stan can be followed on Facebook and Twitter. He can be contacted via www.naturesmart.com.

432